ULTIMATE
BOOK
OF
JOKES

igloo

igloo

Published in 2011
by Igloo Books Ltd
Cottage Farm
Sywell
Northants
NN6 0BJ
www.igloo-books.com

10 9 8 7 6 5

ISBN 978 1 84817 238 8

Project Management by Metro Media Ltd

Compiler: Samantha Wallis
Text Design & Layout: Andy Huckle
Cover design: JHX
Illustrations: Clipart.com

Contents

What do you get when you cross a cow with a grass cutter?
A lawn moo-er

What do you call a pig that does karate?
Pork chop

What says, "Cluck, baa, moo, quack, oink, neigh"?
A multilingual chicken

How do you con a sheep?
Pull the wool over its eyes

What do you get if you cross a duck with a firework?
A firequacker

Why did the chicken cross the road?
To get to the other side

Why did the duck cross the road?
To prove it wasn't chicken

Why did the turkey cross the road?
The chicken was on holiday

Why did the cow cross the road?
To get to the udder side

What do cows play at parties?
Moo-sical chairs

What do you call a headless sheep with no legs?
A cloud

Where did the bull take the cow on their first date?
The moo-vies

Where would you take a poorly pony?
Horse-pital

What do you call a chicken that tells jokes?
A comedi-hen

Why did the pony cough?
He was a little horse

Knock, knock
Who's there?
Cows
Cows who?
No they don't, they moo

What did the vet give the sick pig?
Oink-ment

What do you call a three-legged ass?
A wonkey donkey

What do you call a sleeping bull?
A bull-dozer

What do you call a deer with no eyes?
No eye deer

What do you call a deer with no eyes or legs?
Still no eye deer

Two cows are eating grass in the meadow, when the first cow turns to the other and says, "Are you worried about mad cow disease?" The second cow thinks carefully for a moment before replying, "Of course I'm not, I'm a duck."

What goes "cluck, cluck, bang"?
A chicken crossing a minefield

Where did Duck Lightyear go?
To infinity and the pond

Where do sheep go to get a haircut?
The baa baa's

How do you make milkshake?
Creep up behind the cow and shout "boo"

What happens if you walk under a cow?
You get a pat on the head

What do you call a pig with three eyes?
A piiig

What do you call a pig with no eyes?
A pg

What do you call a pig with a machine gun?
Ham-bo

What do you call a sheep with a machine gun?
Lamb-bo

What do you call a bull with a machine gun?
Whatever he wants you to

Why do cows have bells?
Because their horns don't work

What do you call a cow with no legs?
Ground beef

What are birds' favorite television programmes?
Duck-umentaries

What kind of eggs do evil chickens lay?
Devilled eggs

What do pigs wear with their shirts?
Pigs-ties

Where do American cows live?
Moo York

What did the apple tree say to the farmer?
Stop picking on me

What do you get if you cross a chicken with a cow?
Roost beef

Little birdie flying high dropped a message from the sky
"Oh," said the farmer, wiping his eye, "isn't it good that cows can't fly."

When is ink
like a sheep?
When it's in a pen

What did the farmer
give to the sick chicken?
Tweetment

What did the bull say when he came out of the china shop?
"I've had a smashing time."

Why didn't the piglets listen to their grandfather?
Because he was an old boar

Why did the farmer plough his field with a steam roller?
He wanted to grow mashed potato

Why don't the pigs talk to the chickens?
Because they use fowl language

How do you make ice-cream?
Put a cow in the freezer

What do you get if you cross a duck and a rooster?
A bird that wakes you up at the quack of dawn

What happened to the sheep that swallowed a clock?
It got tics

What do you get if you feed gunpowder to a chicken?
An egg-sposion

What has four legs and says "boo"?
A cow with a cold

Why do horses wear shoes?
Because they can't find boots that fit

What do you get if you cross a teddy with a pig?
A teddy boar

What kind of bird lays electric eggs?
A battery hen

What says "quick, quick"?
A duck with hiccups

What do you get if you cross a chicken and a cement mixer?
A brick layer

Is chicken soup good for your health?
Not if you're a chicken

What do sheep enjoy on sunny days?
A baa-baa-cue

Why did the farmer give his chickens whiskey?
He wanted them to lay Scotch eggs

Why did the scarecrow win an award?
Because he was outstanding in his field

Knock, knock!
Who's there?
Farmer
Farmer who?
Farmer distance you look much smaller

Why did the farmer take some hay to bed?
To feed his nightmares

Why was the turkey the drummer in the band?
He had his own drumsticks

Where do old cows live?
In a moo-seum

Why didn't the farmer say thank you to the pigs?
He took them for grunted

How many sheep does it take to make a sweater?
I didn't know sheep could knit

Why did the horse cross the road?
He wanted to visit his neigh-bors

Why did the farmer sleep under his tractor?
He needed to wake up oily

What's an ambush?
A tree with pigs growing on it

Why did Sampson sleep with his shoes on?
Because he was a horse

How did the rambler hurt the farmer?
He trod on his corn

Why did the farmer call his pig Ink?
Because it was always running out of the pen

Which side of a chicken has most feathers?
The outside

Why are cows not good dancers?
They have two left feet

What do you call a cow that doesn't produce milk?
An udder failure

Where do cows go to dance?
Meatballs

How do cattle do maths?
With a cow-culator

Knock, knock.
Who's there?
Interrupting cow.
Interrupting c...
Mooooo!

What did the daddy chicken say to his naughty son?
Cock-a-doodle-don't do that

What do you get if you cross a chicken and a skunk?
A fowl smell

Why did the chicken cross the road?
To prove it had guts

How do chickens know when to get up in the morning?
They use an alarm cluck

Who was the pig writing to?
His pen friend

13

Why do cows lie down when it rains?
To keep each udder dry

Why did the chicken blush?
She was hen-barrassed

What do you get if you cross a
chicken and a dog?
Pooched eggs

What do you call a sheep thief?
A ram raider

What did one pig say to the other?
Shall we be pen pals?

What did the ram say to his girlfriend?
"I love ewe."

What did the dog say to the cow?
Woof

Why don't pigs go on holiday?
They like to sty at home

What key did the cow choir sing in?
Beef flat

How do you arrest a pig?
Put him in ham cuffs

Why did the cow jump over the moon?
The farmer's hands were cold

What did the ram say to the ewe on Valentines Day?
"Wool you be mine?"

How do sheep finish their letters?
"Ewes sincerely."

What do sheep say to each other at Christmas?
"Seasons bleatings."

Why does a milking stool only have three legs?
Because the cow has the udder

Why shouldn't you tell a pig your secrets?
Because they're squealers

How do sheep keep warm in winter?
Central bleating

Why are chickens workaholics?
They work around the cluck

Who wrote 'Great Eggspectations'?
Charles Chickens

What was written on the turkey's gravestone?
Roast in peace

What did the cow say to the comedian?
"Herd any good ones lately?"

What do you call a cow wearing a crown?
A dairy queen

What do you get if you cross some nuns with a chicken?
A pecking order

What do you call a pig with fleas?
Pork scratchings

What do you get if you cross a cow with a crystal ball?
A message from the udder side

How did the farmer mend his trousers?
With cabbage patches

What is a buttress?
A female goat

Knock, knock
Who's there?
Goat
Goat who?
Goat to the door
and you'll find out

What do you call someone who steals pigs?
A ham-burgler

What do you call a chicken in a shell suit?
An egg

What do you call a herd of cows with a sense of humor?
A laughing stock

What is a running chicken?
Poultry in motion

What do you call a goat that lives on a mountain?
A hillbilly

What do you call a clever duck?
A wise quacker

Why are sheep always broke?
They keep getting fleeced

What did the mama chicken say to her naughty chicks?
"Just peck it in."

Why did the clown cross the road?
To find his rubber chicken

How do horses propose?
They go down on bended neigh

What do iron chickens do?
Come home to rust

How do pigs make coffee?
In a porkulator

Which part of a
donkey is the oldest?
Donkey's ears

What do you get from a pampered cow?
Spoiled milk

What grows up and down at the same time?
A duckling

What has five fingers and drives a tractor?
A farm hand

What do you call a pig driving a car?
A road hog

What do you get if you cross a pig with a snake?
A boar constrictor

Why didn't the shepherd cross the road?
Because he was sheepish

Why did the cow cross the road?
Because it was moo-ving house

What did the cow say to her calf when she saw its messy room?
"Were you born in a barn?"

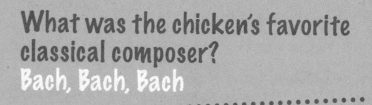

What was the chicken's favorite classical composer?
Bach, Bach, Bach

Why do chickens sit on their eggs?
Because they don't have any chairs

What do you call a quiet sheep?
A shhhhhhhhhhhhhhhh-eep

What did the cow say to the horse?
"Why the long face?"

What does a cow call a fly?
A moo-sance

What did the cow say on Christmas morning?
"Moo-rey Christmas."

How do sheep greet each other at Christmas?
"Merry Christmas to ewe."

What do you call a chicken from outer space?
An eggs-traterrestrial

How do pigs write their top secret messages?
With invisible oink

What do you call a dancing sheep?
A baaaa-llerina

What do you say to a chicken before it goes on stage?
"Break an egg."

What did the winner of the race lose?
Her breath

What do you call a cow with a twitch?
Beef jerky

Why are farmers cruel?
Because they pull the ears off corn

What has ears but can't hear?
Corn

If a rooster lays an egg on a roof, which way will it fall?
It won't, roosters can't lay eggs

How do chickens bake a cake?
From scratch

How does a chicken mail a letter?
In a hen-velope

Why was the bird afraid of the dark?
Because she was a chicken

What does a duck put his cheese on?
Quackers

Where does a peacock go when it loses its tail?
The re-tail store

What did the duck say when it went shopping?
"Put it on my bill."

Did you hear the story about the peacock?
It's a beautiful tail

Why do hens lay eggs?
Because if they dropped them they would break

Why wasn't the rooster rich?
He worked for chicken feed

Why did the chicken go to the doctor?
It had people pox

What do you call a crate of ducks?
A box of quackers

What key won't open a door?
A turkey

What do you get if you cross a chicken with a cow?
Roost beef

How did the farmer count his cattle?
With his cowculator

Why do cows like being told jokes?
They like being amoosed

What do you call an arctic cow?
An eskimoo

What was the pig's favorite ballet?
Swine Lake

Why did the pig go to the casino?
To play the slop machines

What do you get when you cross a sheep with a porcupine?
An animal that knits its own sweaters

Where do sick pigs go?
Hogspital

When is a horse not a horse?
When it turns into a pasture

How did the pig get to the hospital?
In a hambulance

What do you get if you cross a cow and a duck?
Milk and quackers

Why do ducks watch the news?
To see the feather forecast

What happened when the cow jumped over the barbed wire fence?
It was an udder catastrophe

What runs around a farm, but doesn't move?
A fence

If a cow fell into a glass of cola why wouldn't it hurt?
Because cola is a soft drink

Why did the farmer buy a brown cow?
He wanted chocolate milk

Why is it hard to have a conversation with a goat?
Because they are always butting in

What do you get if you cross a pig with a centipede?
Bacon and legs

What did the policeman put on the pig?
Ham cuffs

What do you call a female duck pretending to be a male?
A fake drake

What kind of doctor treats ducks?
A quack

What do you get if you cross a cow with a tadpole?
A bullfrog

What was the cow's favorite James Bond movie?
Dr Moo

What do you call a donkey with one eye and three legs?
A winkey wonkey donkey

What do you call a horse with wheels?
A mustang

What do you get when a cow gets caught in an earthquake?
Milkshake

What do you call a cow that can go in the washing machine?
Washer-bull

What do you call a baby turkey?
A goblet

What do you call a cow that says "baa"?
Bilingual

What do you call an actor who keeps chickens?
Gregory Peck

Why did the girl put a horse on her head?
She wanted a pony tail

What do you call a Scottish horse rider?
Jock Ey

What do you call a vampire pig?
Pork-ula

What do you call a Danish prince with a pig on his head?
Hamlet

Why won't prawns share their sweets?
Because they're shellfish

How do electric eels taste?
Shocking

What happened when the prawn went to the gym?
It pulled a mussel

Why did the starfish blush?
Because it saw the ship's bottom

What does a crab say when it answers the phone?
"Shello."

Why did the octopus have to see the psychiatrist?
Because he was a crazy, mixed-up squid

Why did the crab get arrested?
He kept pinching things

What's yellow and dangerous?
Shark-infested custard

Why was the fish disgusted?
Because the sea weed

How do dolphin's make a decision?
They flipper coin

How do you make a fish keep a secret?
Ask it not to tell a sole

What do you call a fish with no eyes?
Fsh

How do you know when there's a whale in your refrigerator?
You can't shut the door

Why did the shark eat the clock?
He was just killing time

What happened to the ship that sank in shark-infested water?
It came back with a skeleton crew

Which fish do dogs chase?
Catfish

What do you get if you cross an electric eel with a sponge?
Shock absorbers

What happens when you cross a girl jellyfish and a boy jellyfish?
Jelly babies

What do you get if you cross a jellyfish and an elephant?
Jelly the elephant

What kind of bed does a mermaid sleep on?
A water bed

What do you get if you cross an octopus and a skunk?
An octo-pong

What do two octopi do when they are in love?
Walk arm in arm in arm in arm in arm in arm in arm in arm

What game do fish play?
Name that tuna

What do you call a baby whale?
A little squirt

What's the difference between a piano and a fish?
You can tune a piano but you can't tuna fish

What lies at the bottom of the sea and shakes?
A nervous wreck

Where did the sick ship go?
To the docks

How do you sink a submarine full of idiots?
Knock on the door

What part of a fish weighs the most?
The scales

What's the strongest creature in the ocean?
A mussel

What do you call a woman with a beach on her head?
Shelly

What is black and yellow and buzzes along under the sea?
A bee in a submarine

What musical instruments do spanish fishermen play?
Cast-a-nets

What kind of fish can't swim?
Dead ones

What do you get if you cross a shark with a president of the USA?
Jaws Washington

What do you do with crude oil?
Teach it some manners

Why couldn't the ocean sleep?
It had rocks on its bed

Which underwater creature is good at math?
An octo-plus

What did the Pacific Ocean say to the Atlantic Ocean?
Nothing, it just waved

What do you get if you cross a piranha and a nose?
I don't know but I wouldn't pick it

What do you call a fish that performs operations?
A sturgeon

Why didn't the shark eat the woman?
It was a man eater

What sort of fish do you find in a birdcage?
A perch

What sort of fish do you find in a shoe?
An eel

Where did the fish go when he moved?
His new plaice

Knock, knock
Who's there?
Plaice
Plaice who?
Plaice to meet you

Knock, knock
Who's there?
Whale
Whale who?
Whale meet again

Knock, knock
Who's there?
Minnow
Minnow who?
Minnow you're in there

Knock, knock
Who's there?
Piranha
Piranha who?
Piranha kettle, I
need a cup of tea

Knock, knock
Who's there?
Wave
Wave who?
Wave got bored of
waiting, goodbye

What fish light up the sky?
Starfish

What do underwater police drive?
Squid cars

Knock, knock
Who's there?
Kelp
Kelp who?
Kelp me I'm drowning!

What sort of fish go to heaven when they die?
Angel fish

....

Why did the octopus's dinner get cold?
His mum told him to go wash his hands before he ate

....

What eats its prey two by two?
Noah's shark

....

Where did the homeless octopus live?
Squid row

....

What do you get if you cross a flat fish and a bird?
A cheep skate

....

If you had five octopi in your purse what would you be?
Squids in

....

What do you get if you cross shellfish with a rabbit?
The oyster bunny

....

Why are fish bad at tennis?
They don't like getting close to the net

What do you call a whale that can't keep secrets?
A blubber mouth

What happened to the man
who washed up on a purple beach?
He was marooned

Who is the biggest
gangster under the sea?
Al Caprawn

How do fish dry
themselves?
In a fin dryer

What lives under the sea and bites all the fish?
A clampire

How many lighthouse keepers does
it take to change a light bulb?
Twenty – have you seen the size of
a lighthouse bulb?

What never gets any wetter
no matter how much it rains?
The sea

What kind of house weighs
the least?
A lighthouse

How do you catch
a school of fish?
With a bookworm

What holds water
but is full of holes?
A sponge

Who granted the fish's wish?
His fairy cod-mother

What happened to the ray when
it met the great white shark?
It became an x-ray

Who wrote a book called 'How To Catch Sharks'?
Janetta Biggun

What did the lobster call when he wanted to go home?
A taxi crab

What did the dolphin say to the whale when
he bumped into him?
"I'm sorry I didn't do it on porpoise."

Why couldn't the pirates play cards?
Because the captain was standing on the deck

What is the coldest mammal in the world?
The blue whale

What do you call a fish on a table?
A plaice mat

MAN 1: What do you know about the dead sea?
MAN 2: I didn't even know it had been ill

Beach fishing - by C. Shaw

Who held the baby octopus for ransom?
Squidnappers

Who was voted the best-dressed creature in the sea?
The swordfish, because he always looked sharp

Why do sharks live in salt water?
Because pepper water makes them sneeze

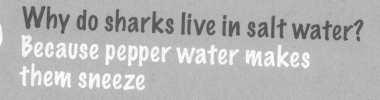

What's the best way to catch a fish?
Have someone throw one to you

Which day of the week do fish hate?
Fry-day

Where did the seaweed find a job?
In the kelp wanted section

Where did the fish go on a date?
The dive-in movie

Why did the fisherman throw peanut butter into the ocean?
To go with the jellyfish

Where did the killer whale go to get his teeth fixed?
The orca-dontist

What kind of ship never sinks?
Friendships

What is a pirate's favorite country?
Arrrrrrrrrrrrrgh-gentina

Where is Captain Hook's treasure chest?
Under his treasure shirt

Why are pirates so bad?
They just arrrrrrgh

Why did Columbus go to jail?
Because he double-crossed the ocean

How do you know the ocean is friendly?
Because it waves

What can run but cannot walk?
Water

What do you wear on the beach?
Sand-als

What kind of hair do oceans have?
Wavy

Why did the ocean roar?
Because it had crabs on its bottom

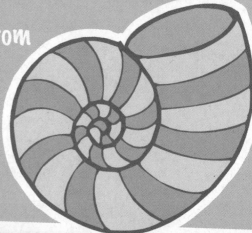

What do you get if you cross a
shark with a parrot?
A bird that talks your ear off

How much did the pirate pay for his earrings?
A buccaneer

What do sea maidens have on their toast?
Merm-alade

Why did the dolphin cross the beach?
To get to the other tide

What makes an octopus laugh?
Ten tickles

If you drop a blue hat in the Red Sea, what does it become?
Wet

What did the fish say when it swam into the wall?
"Dam."

What do you call fish that can't swim?
Dead

What do you call a fish that has eaten 24 carrots?
Goldfish

Why do bears have fur coats?
Because they'd look stupid in anoraks

What's striped and bouncy?
A tiger on a pogo stick

What do you call a bear in a rain storm?
A drizzly bear

What's gray with red spots?
An elephant with measles

Where do crows go for a drink?
A crowbar

What's gray and goes up and down?
An elephant on a trampoline

What's black and white, black and white, black and white?
A zebra on a roundabout

What do you call a lion with toothache?
Rory

What's orange, tastes sweet and swings from trees?
A meringue-utang

Where do monkeys buy their clothes?
Jungle sales

Why do leopards lose at hide and seek?
Because they are always spotted

What is a bear's favorite drink?
Koke-a-Koala

What do polar bears eat for lunch?
Ice burgers

What happened to the leopard who had four baths a day?
After a week he was spotless

What do you get if you cross a tiger with a kangaroo?
A stripy jumper

What animal should you never play cards with?
A cheetah

What do you call a lion who has just eaten your mother's sister?
An aunt-eater

What's the difference between a flea and a wolf?
One prowls on the hairy and one howls on the prairie

Why did the elephant take 6 months to finish the book?
He wasn't very hungry

How does an elephant get down from a tree?
Sits on a leaf and waits until fall

What do you call an elephant who can't spell?
Dumbo

What's a crocodile's favorite game?
Snap

What do you call an elephant witch doctor?
Mumbo jumbo

What do you get when you cross two elephants with a fish?
Swimming trunks

What did the lion say when he saw a skateboarder?
"Meals on wheels."

What's black, white, green, black, white?
Two penguins fighting over a pickle

What black and white and red all over?
A penguin with sunburn

What's large, gray and goes around and around?
An elephant stuck in a revolving door

What's gray and goes up and down, up and down?
An elephant stuck in a lift

How do you make a gorilla cross?
Nail two together

What's black, white, black, white, black, white?
A penguin rolling down a hill

Why isn't there any aspirin in the jungle?
Because the parrots-eat-'em-all

What do you get if you cross a bear with a skunk?
Winnie the Pooh!

Girl: "What's the difference between a bushbaby and a matterbaby?"
Boy: "What's a matterbaby?"
Girl: "Nothing, but it's very sweet of you to ask."

What's yellow and smells of bananas?
Monkey vomit

What did the penguin sing to his friend on his birthday?
"Freeze a jolly good fellow."

What do you call a penguin in the jungle?
Lost

Where did the monkey go when he lost his tail?
The retailer

What did the buffalo's dad say when he went off to college?
"Bison."

First man:
"Have you been out hunting bear?"
Second man:
"No, I was wearing my trousers."

Why shouldn't you take a bear to the zoo?
Because he would rather go bowling

Where do elephants go on vacation?
Tusk-any

How do you get down from a camel?
You don't get down from a camel, you get it from a duck

How do you know if an elephant's been in your refrigerator?
Footprints in the butter

How do you get an elephant in the refrigerator?
Open the door. Insert elephant. Close the door

How does an elephant get up a tree?
Sits on an acorn and waits for it to grow

How do you get a rhino in the refrigerator?
Open the door. Remove the elephant. Insert rhino. Close the door

Why was the monkey arrested?
The police wanted to gorilla

Why did the zookeeper separate the gnus?
Because he had good gnus and bad gnus

What's the best way to get a wild hippo?
Call it names

What's pink and hard?
A flamingo wearing knuckle dusters

What do you call a camel with three humps?
Humphrey

What do you get if you cross a parrot with a clock?
Polly-tics

How do lions recharge their cell phones?
They plug them into the manes

What happened when the monkey chased the banana?
The banana split

What do you call a bear with no ear?
B

What bird is always out of breath?
A puffin

What's black, white and noisy?
A penguin with a drum kit

Why did the chimp put a burger on his head?
He thought he was a griller

What has antlers and bites?
A moose-quito

Why does a giraffe have such a long neck?
Because its head is a long way from its body

What does a porcupine have for lunch?
Prickled onions

What do you get when you cross a chair with a bird?
A stool pigeon

What did the chimp say when his sister had a baby?
"Well, I'll be a monkey's uncle."

What animal falls from clouds?
Reindeer

Knock, knock
Who's there?
Celia
Celia who?
Celia later, alligator

Why do ostriches have long necks?
Because their feet smell

Why do mother kangaroos hate rainy days?
Because the kids have to play inside

Why do lions eat raw meat?
Because they can't cook

Why are elephants large gray and wrinkly?
Because if they were small, brown and furry then they would be mice

What do you call an elephant in a letterbox?
Stuck

Why are elephants wrinkly?
Because they don't fit on the ironing board

What did the leopard say after his meal?
"That hit the spots."

What smells like bananas?
Monkey farts

What sounds like a parrot?
A carrot

Why is the desert lion everyone's favorite at Christmas?
Because he has sandy claws

What smells like eucalyptus?
Koala farts

Why did the elephant paint the soles of his feet yellow?
So he could hide upside-down in a bowl of custard

Did you ever find an elephant in your custard?
Must work then!

Why is it hard to play cards in the jungle?
There are too many cheetahs

What is black and white and pink all over?
A hypno-potomus

What do you call a sick reptile?
An illagator

What do you get if you cross a monkey with a firework?
A baboom

Why did the armadillo cross the road?
It didn't get run over

There were ten monkeys in the zoo,
and all but nine escaped. How many were left?
Nine

What did the lion eat in the restaurant?
The waiter

Why did the snake go to war?
He was coiled up

Why do elephants have big ears?
Because Noddy wouldn't pay the ransom

What do you call an aardvark with two black eyes and a broken nose?
A vark

What do you get if you cross a bird with a snake?
A feather boa constrictor

What do you do when a herd of elephants is running toward you?
Make a trunk call and reverse the charges

What's the definition of an aardvark?
A vark that thinks it's tough

What is out of bounds?
A tired kangaroo

Do crocodiles snore?
Only when they're asleep

What is a polygon?
A dead parrot

What fur do you get from a tiger?
As fur away as possible

How do you know if there is an elephant in your bed?
He has a big E on his pyjamas

Whats big, gray and puts you in a trance?
A hypno-potomus

What's worse than a giraffe with a sore throat?
An elephant with a runny nose

What looks like an elephant and can fly?
A flying elephant

Why did the elephant take a shower?
Because he couldn't fit into the bath

How do you fix a broken chimp?
With a monkey wrench

What did the banana say to the monkey?
Nothing, bananas can't talk

What kind of fruit do you get from an angry gorilla?
Grrrrrrr-ape

What is big,
gray and
wobbles?
A jello-phant

Why were the bears kissing?
They were going teddy

What is a prickly pear?
Two porcupines

Why was the bear on the run?
He was wan-ted

What sort of dog has no tail and no legs?
A hotdog

Why can't a giraffe stand on its head?
Because it's too high up

Why do elephants wear sandals?
To stop them sinking into the sand

Which elephant never gets wet?
An umbrella-phant

Why do ostriches bury their heads in the sand?
They're looking for the elephants who didn't wear sandals

Why can't penguins keep secrets at the north pole?
Because their teeth keep chattering

Why don't koalas wear shoes?
They like walking in bear feet

What's black and white and eats like a horse?
A zebra

Why are giraffes brave?
They're always sticking their neck out

What type of monkey can fly?
A hot air baboon

Why are anteaters good workers?
Because a little aardvark never hurt anyone

What is a sheep's favorite sport?
Baaaaadminton

What animal is made from wood?
A timber wolf

What do yaks talk about?
The latest gnus

What is a wallaby's favorite arcade game?
Mortal Wombat

What's gray, has wings and a wand?
The tusk fairy

What do you get if you cross a
hyena and gravy?
A laughing stock

What do you get if you cross a zebra and a pelican?
Over the road safely

What do you get if you put a bear in the freezer?
A teddy brrr

What do you call a drunk rhino?
A wino

What do you call a monkey with a bomb?
A baboom

What do you call a hippo without a tail?
A hippobottomless

Why did the tortoise cross the road?
I don't know, it's not got to the other side yet

Do you see penguins on safaris?
Not safaris I know

What do you call a pale teddy bear?
Wan-ted

What do you call a tanned teddy bear?
Unwan-ted

What do you call a happy teddy bear?
Content-ted

Why are alligators quick witted?
Because they always give snappy answers

What is black, white and red all over?
An embarrassed zebra

What's black and white and has wheels?
A penguin on a skateboard

Why did the wolf cross the road?
He wanted to eat the chicken

Why did the stag wear braces?
He had buck teeth

Which animal has a lot of gas?
An aard-fart

What is an ape's favorite cookie?
Chocolate chimp

What do you call a tiger with no stripes?
A lion

What is a reptile's favorite movie?
The Lizard of Oz

What goes ha ha ha plop?
A hyena laughing his head off

What do you get if you cross a jaguar with an elephant?
A car with a big trunk

Why don't leopards go on vacation?
They can't find the right spot

What do you get when you cross a cheetah with a hamburger?
Fast food

Why did the lion eat the tightrope walker?
He wanted a balanced meal

Why does the elephant use his trunk as a bookmark?
So he always nose where he stopped reading

What happened when the goose got cold?
She got people bumps

How do porcupines play leap frog?
Carefully

What is the highest form of animal life?
A giraffe

Why are giraffes slow to apologize?
It takes them a long time to swallow their pride

What did the porcupine say to the cactus?
"Mom?"

Why did the monkey cross the road?
To get the banana on the other side

Is it hard to spot a leopard?
No, they already come like that

What did the aardvark have on his pizza?
Ant-chovies

Where do polar bears keep their money?
In a snow bank

What is 500lb and wears glass slippers?
Cinderellaphant

Why do elephants paint their toenails red?
So they can hide in the strawberry patch

What has six legs, four ears, three trunks and five tusks?
An elephant with spare parts

Why do elephants have gray skin?
To keep their insides together

What should you do with a red elephant?
Stop embarrassing it

What should you do with a yellow elephant?
Teach it to be brave

What should you do with a blue elephant?
Cheer it up

What's black and white and red all over?
A zebra wearing too much lipstick

What did the idiot call his pet zebra?
Spot

How much is a skunk worth?
One scent

Why didn't the lady run away from the lion?
It was a man-eating lion

Zoo visitor: What's the new baby hippo's name?
Hippopotamus keeper: I don't know, he won't tell me

What do you use to paint a dromedary?
Camel enamel

What do you call a fat chimp?
A chunky monkey

What's big, gray, brings you flowers and cheers you up?
A get well-ephant

What's gray and goes round and round?
An elephant in a washing machine

What's big, gray and has 16 wheels?
An elephant on rollerskates

What's the difference between an elephant and a banana?
Have you ever tried to peel an elephant?

What's the difference between an African elephant and an Indian elephant?
About 3,000 miles

What's as big as an elephant but weighs nothing?
An elephant's shadow

What do koalas wear when its raining?
Gumboots

What disguise did the elk wear?
A false moose-tache

Why did the two elephants get chucked out of the swimming pool?
Because they only had a pair of trunks between them

What do you call a rubbish lion tamer?
Claude Bottom

What do you call someone who is part man part jungle cat?
Richard the Lion Half

Why did the cross-eyed teacher get the sack?
He couldn't control his pupils

Why is history like fruitcake?
It's full of dates

Why did the bird fly into the library?
It was looking for bookworms

Teacher: If you had $1 and asked your mother
for another $1 then how much would you have?"
Pupil: "$1, sir."
Teacher: "You don't know you arithmetic."
Pupil: "You don't know my mother!"

Why are art galleries like retirement homes for teachers?
They're both full of old masters

Did you hear the one about the brilliant geography teacher?
He had abroad knowledge of his subject

What's black when it's clean and white when it's dirty?
A blackboard

Why did the teacher turn the lights on?
Because the class was so dim

How many letters are there in the alphabet?
11 – T-H-E A-L-P-H-A-B-E-T

When did nerds rule the world?
In the dork ages

Dad: "Would you like me to help you with your homework?"
Son: "No thanks, I'd rather get it wrong all by myself."

Teacher: "If you had $20 in one pocket and $30 in the other pocket, what would you have?"
Boy: "Somebody else's trousers."

Why did the teacher wear sunglasses?
Because her class was so bright

What did the music teacher call her daughters?
Carol and Melody

Teacher: "Who can tell me where Hadrian's Wall is?"
Pupil: "Around his garden, sir?"

Why were the early days of history called the dark ages?
Because there were so many knights

What kind of food do math teachers eat?
Square meals

Why was the math book worried?
Because it had so many problems

What do history teachers do before they get married?
Go out on dates

Why was the schoolboy locked in a cage?
He was the teacher's pet

Boy: "I can't play soccer today, sir, I've sprained my ankle."
Teacher: "That's a lame excuse."

Dinner lady: "Your school dinners are full of iron."
Boy: "Is that why they're so chewy?"

What happens when witches and wizards break the school rules?
They are ex-spelled

Where do skinny teachers train?
Puney-versity

Where do music teachers train?
Tune-iversity

Where do mad teachers train?
Looney-versity

Where do alien teachers train?
Moon-iversity

What happened to the boy who messed around in music class?
He got into treble

Boy: "Sir, when I grow up, I want to be a pilot."
Teacher: "You've got your head in the clouds boy."

Teacher: "That's an excellent essay for someone your age."
Pupil: "What about someone my mums age, sir?"

Pupil: "What do you mean my spelling's no good? That's my algebra."

Mother: "How is my son doing at school?"
Principal: "He can speak three different languages."
Mother: "Really?"
Principal: "Yes, double Dutch, utter gibberish and complete twaddle."

What did the music teacher do when he was off sick?
Sent in a note

Teacher: "Why did the Romans build straight roads?"
Pupil: "Because they didn't have steering wheels on their chariots, sir."

What happens to old math teachers?
They are taken away

Teacher: "Has you father been helping you with your homework?"
Pupil: "No sir, he did it all by himself."

Knock, knock
Who's there
Teacher
Teacher who?
Teacher self I've had enough

What do you get if you cross the science department with a dog?
A lab

Boy: "Sorry I'm late sir, I overslept."
Teacher: "You mean you sleep at home too?"

Teacher: "Do you understand how important punctuation is?"
Pupil: "Yes, I always arrive at school on time, sir."

Mother: "What makes you think my John's a truant?"
Teacher: "John? there's no John in this school."

Why did the school orchestra have such bad manners?
It didn't know how to conduct itself

Why didn't the math teacher's plant grow?
Because it had square roots

Girl: "My brother is the school swot."
Boy: "Is he very clever?"
Girl: "No ,just good at killing flies."

Teacher: "You aren't paying attention boy, are you having trouble hearing?"
Boy: "No sir, I'm having trouble listening."

Father: "Do you like going to school son?"
Son: "The going bit is alright and so is the coming home, it's the bit in the middle I don't like much."

Girl: "Our teacher talks to himself, what about yours?"
Boy: "Yes, but she doesn't realize it, she actually thinks we're listening."

Playing truant from school is like a credit card
Fun now, pay later

What's the definition of an archeologist?
Someone whose career is in ruins

What has forty feet and sings?
The school choir

Teacher: "What does coincidence mean?"
Boy: "That's funny I was going to ask you the same thing."

Why is six afraid of seven?
Because seven eight nine

Who invented fractions?
Henry the 1/8th

What animal is best at math? Rabbits because they're good at multiplying

What kind tree did the math teacher plant in her garden? A geome-tree

Boy: "I got 100 in math today and still didn't pass."
Mother: "Why didn't you pass?"
Boy: "The answer was 200."

Teacher: "If I had six apples in one hand and ten apples in the other had what would I have?"
Girl: "Huge hands, sir."

Teacher: "John, I hope I didn't see you copying Jack's work."
John: "I hope you didn't either, sir."

Teacher: "Give me a sentence with the words defence, defeat and detail in it."
Boy: "When the horse jumped over defence, defeat went before detail."

Teacher: "Simon, can you spell your name backwards?"
Simon: "No mis."

Teacher: "What is the most common sentence used in school?"
Boy: "I don't know."
Teacher: "Correct."

Father: "What did you learn in school today?"
Son: "Not enough, I have to go back tomorrow."

What two letters are always jealous?
N-V

Boy: "I think my teacher loves me."
Mother: "Why do you say that?"
Boy: "She keeps putting Xs on my work."

What letter is always wet?
C

Mother: "What did you learn at school today?"
Girl: "How to write."
Mother: "What did you write?"
Girl: "I don't know, they're not teaching us how to read until next week."

What's the laziest letter of the alphabet?
E because it's always in bed

Which letter of the alphabet is always asking questions?
Y

Daughter: "Dad can you write in the dark?"
Father: "Yes I think so, what do you want me to write on?"
Daughter: "My report card."

Mother: "Why did you swallow that money?"
Son "You said it was my lunch money."

How do you spell 80 with just two letters?
A-T

What did the zero say to the eight?
"Nice belt."

Why did the girl eat her homework?
Because the teacher told her it was a piece of cake

"I'm sorry to tell you that your teacher has fallen down a wishing well."
"Yes! It works."

What's the most important thing to remember in chemistry?
Don't lick the spoon

Why did the boy slip on the library floor?
He was in the non-friction section

What has a spine but no bones?
A book

What were 20 schoolboys playing in a phone booth?
Squash

What do you get if you cross a math teacher with a piece of furniture?
A multiplication table

Girl: "Girls are smarter than boys."
Boy: "I didn't know that."
Girl: "See what I mean."

Teacher: "Are you sleeping in my class?"
Boy: "Not any more, sir."

Son: "Dad, will you do my homework for me?"
Father: "No son, that wouldn't be right."
Son: "It won't be right if I do it either."

Teacher: "What's the difference between ignorance and apathy?"
Boy: "I don't know and I don't care."

Why shouldn't you bring a piranha to class?
Because they attack in schools

Teacher: "Who was the Roman queen of the gods?"
Girl: "Juno, sir."
Teacher: "Of course I do, but I'm asking you."

Librarian: "How many books have you read in your lifetime?"
Boy: "I don't know, I'm not dead yet."

What do you call someone who keeps on talking when nobody's listening any more?
Teacher

Teacher: "Why are you doing your sums on the floor?"
Boy: "Because you told me to do it without using tables sir."

Teacher: "Give me two pronouns."
Boy: "Who, me?"
Teacher: "Correct."

Teacher: "Why is your writing so untidy?"
Boy: "So you can't spot my spelling mistakes."

Teacher: "How many days of the week start with the letter T?"
Pupil: "Four. Tuesday, Thursday, today and tomorrow."

Teacher: "Who started the fight?"
Boy: "He did sir, he punched me back on purpose."

When are school uniforms a fire danger?
When they're blazers

What do elves learn at school?
The elf-abet

What did the math book say to the reading book?
Don't tell me your sob stories I'm the one with problems

Teacher: "Give me a sentence beggining with the letter I."
Girl: "I is..."
Teacher: "No, always say 'I am'."
Girl: "Alright, I am the ninth letter of the alphabet."

Teacher: "If 'can't' is short for 'cannot' what is 'don't' short for?"
Boy: "Doughnut."

My teacher has a sympathetic face. Every time I look at it I feel sympathy for her

How do religious education teachers mark exam papers?
They use spirit levels

Teacher: "This essay you wrote about a dog is exactly the same as your brother's."
Girl: "Well, it's the same dog, sir."

Teacher: "Recite me your tables."
Boy: "Kitchen table, bedside table, dining table..."

Dad: "What did you learn at school today son?"
Son: "I learned that you can't do math."

Why are math teachers good at dancing?
Because they've got logarithms

If two's company and three's a crowd, what are four and five?
Nine

What does everyone have that they can always count on?
Fingers

What do moths study at school?
Mothematics

What did one book say to the other?
Page me

How do you become a professor?
By degrees

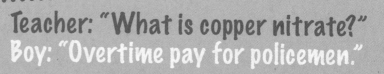

What did the electrician say to his son
when he was late home from school?
"Wire you insulate?"

Teacher: "What is copper nitrate?"
Boy: "Overtime pay for policemen."

What is a bookworm's idea of a big feast?
War and Peace

Which word in the dictionary is spelled incorrectly?
Incorrectly

What happens once in a minute, twice in a moment,
but never in a hundred years?
The letter M

How do bees get to school?
On the school buzz

Teacher: "What is the centre of gravity?"
Boy: "V, sir."

How do you get straight A's?
Use a ruler

Why was the broom late for school?
It overswept

What book has hair?
The diction-hairy

What do you get when you cross a library and an elf?
A shhhhh-elf

What is bigger when it's upside down?
6

How did the music teacher get locked out of the classroom?
She left her keys in the piano

Why did the music teacher need a ladder?
To reach the high notes

How is an english teacher like a judge?
They both hand out sentences

How did the science teacher freshen his breath?
With experi-mints

Why was the teacher's head wet?
He had a brainstorm

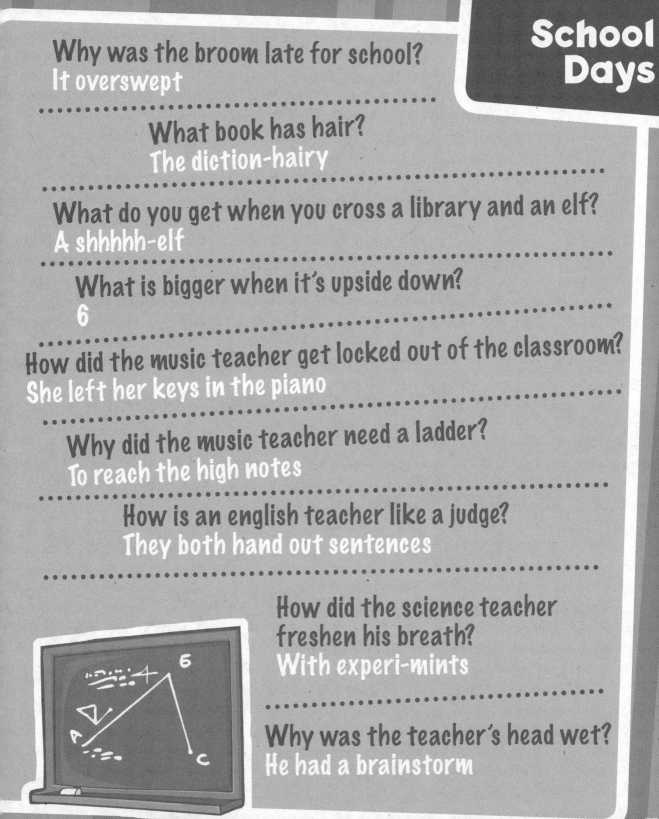

What did the limestone say to the geologist?
Don't take me for granite

Who writes invisible books?
A ghost writer

Where did the librarian sleep?
Between the covers

What do you call someone whose library books are overdue?
A bookkeeper

What has wings and solves number problems?
A moth-matician

Where do math teachers go sight seeing?
Times Square

Why did the boy bring a ladder to school?
He thought it was high school

If a dictionary goes from A-Z
What goes from Z-A?
Zebra

Why did the scientist have a knocker on his door?
He wanted to win the no-bell prize

Which book is about chickens?
The hen-cyclopedia

What kind of building is the tallest in the world?
The library, as it has the most stories

Why did the schoolboy throw a glass of water out the window?
He wanted to see a waterfall

What do you call a man with this book on his head?
Joe King

What's the smartest American state?
Alabama because it has 4 As and 1 B

Teacher: "Why don't you answer me?"
Pupil: "I did sir, I shook my head."
Teacher: "Well, you don't expect me to hear it rattling from here do you?"

What did the mouse say to the camera?
"Cheese."

What's a cat's favorite dessert?
Mice pudding

Where do Dutch hamsters live?
Hamster-dam

What you get if a budgie flies into a blender?
Shredded tweet

What do you get if you cross a cat with a parrot?
A carrot

What do you call a cat that has just eaten a duck?
A duck-filled fatty puss

Why did the dog say "baa"?
It was learning a new language

What is Lassie's favorite flower?
A collie flower

Why did the dog go to see the vet?
He was feeling ruff

Where did the cat cross the road?
At the purr-destrian crossing

Where would you find a dog with no legs?
Exactly where you left it

What's furry, has four legs and a suitcase?
A dog going on vacation

What happens when you shout at a cat?
You hurt its felines

Lady: "My cat thinks it's a chicken."
Man: "Why don't you take it to the vet?"
Lady: "We need the eggs."

What's worse than raining cats and dogs?
Raining elephants

What's a cat's favorite take-away?
Egg-fried mice

What do you get if you pour boiling
water down a rabbit hole?
A hot, cross bunny

How do you stop your dog barking in the hallway?
Put him in the kitchen

What do you get if you cross a dog with some soil?
A Land Rover

Poster in a pet shop: Special offer this week. Buy one cat, get one flea!

First man: "My dog has no nose."
Second man: "How does he smell?"
First man: "Awful."

What do you call a cat with a frog on its head?
Lily

Girl: "I've lost my dog."
Boy: "Why don't you put a notice in the newspaper?"
Girl: "Don't be silly, dogs can't read."

Why do hamsters carry their food in their cheeks?
Because they don't have any pockets

What do you call a row of rabbits walking backwards?
A receding hare line

What do you get if you cross a rabbit with a frog?
A ribbit

What has six eyes but can't see?
Three blind mice

What's small, furry and smells of bacon?
A ham-ster

What did the baby mouse say when she saw a bat for the first time?
"I've just seen an angel."

Why did the dog get thrown out of the butcher's shop?
He was chop-lifting

When is it unlucky to see a black cat?
When you're a mouse

What do cats eat for breakfast?
Mice Krispies

Why are cats such good singers?
They're very mew-sical

First man: "My parrot lays square eggs."
Second man: "That's amazing. Can it talk too?"
First man: "Yes, but only one word."
Second man: "What's that?"
First man: "Ouch!"

What goes "dot, dot, dash, squeak"?
Mouse code

Why did the mouse need oiling?
It was sqeaky

What do cats put in their lemonade?
Mice cubes

What do you get if you cross a dog with a clock?
A watchdog

What do you give a dog with a temperature?
Mustard – it's the best thing for a hot dog

How do you know that carrots are good for your eyes?
Have you ever seen a rabbit in glasses?

What do you get if you cross a cat and a lemon?
A sour puss

Why can't you milk a mouse?
The bucket won't fit underneath

What's the most boring breed of dog?
The dull-mation

What do you get if you cross a dog and a cat?
An animal that chases itself

How do you spell mousetrap with just three letters?
C-A-T

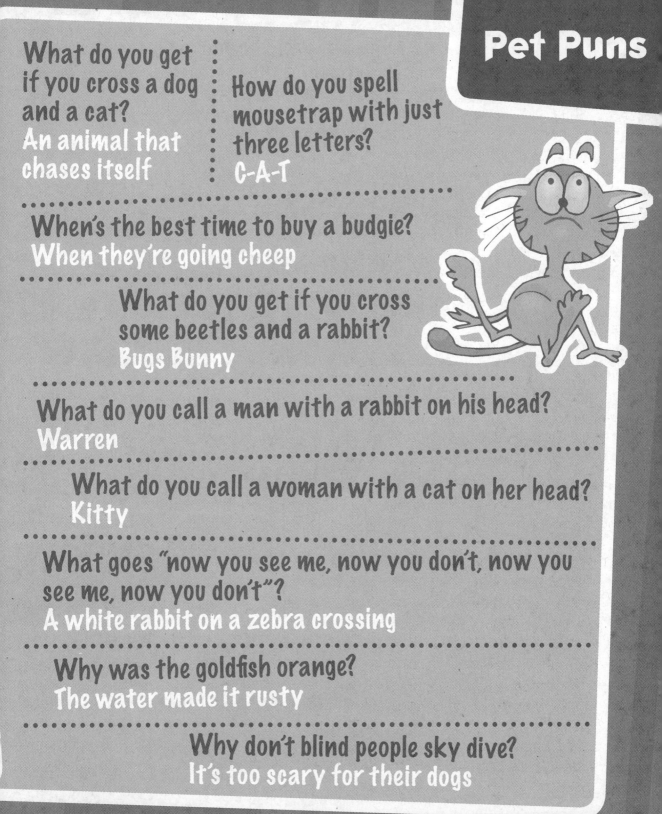

When's the best time to buy a budgie?
When they're going cheep

What do you get if you cross some beetles and a rabbit?
Bugs Bunny

What do you call a man with a rabbit on his head?
Warren

What do you call a woman with a cat on her head?
Kitty

What goes "now you see me, now you don't, now you see me, now you don't"?
A white rabbit on a zebra crossing

Why was the goldfish orange?
The water made it rusty

Why don't blind people sky dive?
It's too scary for their dogs

Why did the dog bury his bone?
He'd forgotten the combination for the safe

How do cats shop?
From a cat-alogue

What do dogs say to each other before they eat?
"Bone appetit"

What happened when the dog went to the flea circus?
It stole the show

What says "krab krab"?
A dog barking at itself in the mirror

What do you call a man with an angry cat on his head?
Claude

What was the cat's favorite song?
Three Blind Mice

Why did the cat get ten out of ten?
It was purr-fect

What sort of cat do you
need in an emergency?
A first aid kitty

"How many dogs does it take to put in a light bulb?"
Rottweiler: Go Ahead! Make me!

How do you make mice smell nice?
Use mousewash

Where did the rabbit learn to fly?
In the hare force

What was the canary doing in prison?
It was a jail bird

What do you call frozen mice?
Micicles

What do you call a dog that thinks it's a sheep?
Baaaaarking mad

What did the mouse say when it broke its teeth?
"Hard cheese."

What do angry rodents send at Christmas?
Cross mouse cards

How do dogs send messages?
Pedigree-mail

What do you call a rabbit that's won the lottery?
A millionhare

What do you get if you cross dog and a vegetable?
A jack brussel

What do you get if you cross a gundog with a maze?
A lab-yrinth

What's the difference between a dog with fleas and a bored guest?
One's going to itch and the others itching to go

Knock, knock
Who's there?
Aware
Aware who?
Aware, aware has my little dog gone?

What do you call a dog with a cold?
Achoo-huahua

What do you call a Scottish parrot?
A macaw

What do you call a rabbit on a diet?
Thinning hare

What do you call a mouse with no legs?
Cat food

What do you call a dog that digs up bones?
A barkyologist

How is cat food sold?
Purr can

"Did you put the cat out?"
"I didn't know it was on fire!"

What do you call a dog that gets mail?
A labrador receiver

What happened to the cat that drank 50 saucers of milk?
It got the lap record

When is a brown dog not a brown dog?
When it's a greyhound

How do you know when your cat has eaten a duck?
It looks down in the mouth

Did you hear about the dog that ran 100 miles to get a stick?
It's a bit farfetched

What happened to the man who went to the fancy dress party as a bone?
The dog buried him in the garden

Girl: "Do you have any dogs going cheap?"
Shop owner: "No, they all say woof."

Which breed of cat purrs the most?
Purrsians

How can you write rabbit without using the letter R?
Bunny

What do you call a rodent with a sword?
A mousekateer

How do you tell the difference between a rabbit and a wooly mammoth?
Try getting a wooly mammoth into a rabbit hutch

Who wrote a book called 'How To Feed Your Dog'?
Nora Bone

What did the budgie say when it's new cage fell apart?
"Cheap cheap."

What do you get when you cross a rottweiler and a collie?
A dog that bites your arm off then goes to get help

Did you hear about the cat that was stolen?
It was taken by a purr-snatcher

What is the loudest pet?
A trum-pet

Why did the dog go to court?
He had a barking ticket

What did the rabbit give his girlfriend?
A 14-carrot ring

What was the dog's favorite color?
Grrrrrrreen

Why did the cat go to sleep in the fireplace?
Because she wanted to sleep like a log

What kind of rabbit drinks coffee?
Mugs bunny

What do you get if you cross a canary with a 50-foot snake?
A sing-a-long

What is a rabbit's favorite music?
Hip hop

What did the 500lb canary say?
Here kitty, kitty

"I'd like to buy some birdseed."
"How many birds do you have?"
"None, I'd like to grow some."

Why didn't the dog like the sea?
There was something fishy about it

What do you get if you cross a spaniel, poodle and rooster?
A cocker-poodle-doo

What do you get if you cross rabbits and ants?
Bugs bunnies

What kind of cats go bowling?
Alley cats

What happened when 500 hares got loose?
The police had to comb the area

Where do mice keep their boats?
At the hickory dickory dock

What do rabbits use to keep their fur in place?
Hare-spray

If a fire hydrant has h2o on the inside, what does it have on the outside?
K9p

What do you call a fake horse?
A phony pony

What do you call a rabbit comedian?
A funny bunny

What do you call a cat comedian?
A witty kitty

Why do cats have fur balls?
Because they love a good gag

What do you call it when a cat bites?
Catnip

What's the worst type of cat to have?
A catastrophe

What do you gat if you cross a cat with a tree?
A cat-a-log

What do you call parrot food?
Polly-filler

What do you call a cat with eight legs that likes to swim?
An octo-puss

Why was the cat so small?
She only drank condensed milk

What do you get if you cross a dog with a cheetah?
A dog that chases cars and catches them

Why should you be careful when it's raining cats and dogs?
You could step in a poodle

What do you get if you cross a dog and a lion?
A terrified postman

What kind of dog wears glasses?
A cock-eyed spaniel

What did the dalmation say after it ate its dinner?
That hit the spots

Why do dogs wag their tails?
Because no-one else will do it for them

How does Mickey feel when Minnie is mad at him?
Mouserable

What dog you call a dog that's out in the snow?
A chilli dog

Where did the newly-wed rabbits go?
On bunnymoon

What do you call a dog that does experiments?
A lab-rador

What do you call a dog that makes a bolt for the door?
Blacksmith

What flower grows on your face?
Two-lips

What's brown and sticky?
A stick

What did the tree say to the axe?
"I'm stumped."

The rain makes all things beautiful,
The grass and flowers too.
If rain makes all things beautiful,
Why won't it rain on you?

Which birds are always sad?
Bluebirds

Why do all the birds in the nest get along?
Because they don't want to fall out

What's a frog's favorite flower?
A croak-us

Why is grass dangerous?
It's full of blades

What did the confused owl say?
To-whit-to-why?

How can you recognize a dogwood tree?
By its bark

Knock, knock
Who's there?
Owl
Owl who?
Owl be angry if you don't let me in

How do you get a one-armed idiot out of a tree?
Wave to him

What do you call a woodpecker with no beak?
A head-banger

What is a bird's favorite part of the news?
The feather forecast

Where do bees go on holiday?
Sting-apore

Why do birds fly south in the winter?
Because it's too far to walk

What kind of tree has hair?
A fur tree

What do you call a man with turf on his head?
Pete

What does Santa use to weed his garden?
His hoe hoe hoe

How many chestnuts grow on the average oak tree?
None, chestnuts don't grow on oak trees

Why should you be careful about telling secrets in a vegetable garden?
Because corn has ears, potatoes have eyes and beanstalk

Why is the river lazy?
It's never out of its bed

....

What kind of bean doesn't grow in the garden?
A jellybean

....

Knock, knock
Who's there?
Leaf
Leaf who?
Leaf me alone

....

When are flowers like underwear?
When they are bloomers

....

What do you get if you cross a genius with a tree?
Albert Pine-stien

....

What do you call a man with a tree
growing out of his head?
Edwood

....

What kind of flower barks?
A dog rose

What gets smaller the more you put in it?
A hole in the ground

....

Why was the garden so bright?
It had a lot of bulbs in it

....

What do trees and dogs have in common?
Bark

....

How do you stop moles digging up your lawn?
Lock the tool shed

....

Where did the bird invest its money?
On the stork market

....

What was the sparrows favorite arcade game?
Tweet Fighter

....

Father: "I'll teach you to throw stones at the greenhouse."
Son: "It's alright dad, I already know how to do it."

Why was the ground greasy?
Because the rain was dripping

Why did the gardener only wear one glove?
Because the weather forecast said it could be sunny
but on the other hand it could be cold

Did you hear about the gardener's children?
One's a blooming idiot, but the other is a budding genius

What do you call well-behaved fog?
Non-confor-mist

Why are rocks ungrateful?
They take everything for granite

What do you call a tree that
will fit in your hand?
A palm

It's really busy work in the garden,
things keep cropping up

Why did the tree dye its hair?
Its roots were showing

What type of tree gets ill the most?
A sycamore

Why did the gardener plant gold?
He wanted rich soil

Why is the sky so high?
So that birds don't bump their heads

What do clouds wear underneath their clothes?
Thunderwear

What do you call a Russian gardener?
Ivanhoe

What did the gardener with the winning poker hand say?
"Weed 'em and reap."

What bug tells the time?
A clock-roach

What kind of bird works on a building site?
A crane

What do you call two spiders that just got married?
Newlywebs

How did the firefly start the race?
"Ready, steady, glow."

How do you tell which end of a worm is its head?
Tickle it and see which end smiles

How do trees get onto the internet?
They log on

What's green and pecks at trees?
Woody wood-pickle

What type of birds stick together?
Vel-crows

What did the alien say to the plant?
"Take me to your weeder."

What is a tree's favorite drink?
Root beer

What type of cookies do birds like?
Chocolate chirp

Which bird do you eat with every meal?
A swallow

What do you get when you cross a bird with an elephant?
A broken bird table

What did the big flower say to the little flower?
"How are you bud?"

What do you call a piece of wood with nothing to do?
Bored

What is a tree's favorite fruit?
Pine-apple

What kind of garden does a baker have?
A flour garden

Why did the gardener plant seeds in the pond?
He wanted to grow watermelons

How does a rose ride a bike?
By pushing the petals

What did the tree wear to the pool?
Swimming trunks

What did the snowman put over his baby's crib?
A snowmobile

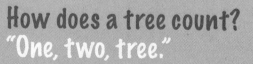

How does a tree count?
"One, two, tree."

What do you call a snowman in the summer?
A puddle

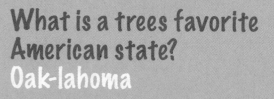

What is a trees favorite American state?
Oak-lahoma

What kind of tree has fingers?
A palm tree

What month do trees dislike?
Sep-timber

What do flowers wear?
Petal pushers

Why didn't the tree like playing checkers?
It was a chess-nut

What books do owls like to read?
Hoot dunnits

If April showers bring May flowers, what do May flowers bring?
Pilgrims

What do bees do with their honey?
They cell it

What do you get if you cross a rose with a crocodile?
I don't know, but I wouldn't try sniffing it

How do you send a message in a forest?
By moss code

What vegetable do you get when a
dinosaur walks through your garden?
A squash

When does it rain money?
When there is a change in the weather

What did the tree say
to the woodcutter?
"Leaf me alone."

What did the dirt say when
it started to rain?
"If this keeps up my name's
gonna be mud."

What flower lies down?
A lazy daisy

What was the bee's favorite movie?
The Sting

What does the queen bee do
when she burps?
Issues a royal pardon

How do you catch a unique bird?
U-neek up on him

How do you catch a tame bird?
The tame way

Knock, knock
Who's there?
Beezer
Beezer who?
Beezer yellow and black

Why did the snail cross the road?
To get to the shell station

What is the queen's favorite weather?
Reign

Knock, knock
Who's there?
Lettuce
Lettuce who?
Lettuce in,
it's cold out here

What do you call a girl with one
foot either side of the river?
Bridget

What do you call something
purple that swings through
your vineyard?
Tarzan the grapeman

What do you call a
naughty cranefly?
Baddy long legs

What happened to the rhubarb thief?
He was taken into custardy

What do you call a
man with a spade
on his head?
Doug

What do you call a man
with flowers growing on
his head?
Gordon

How did the man feel after he got run over?
Tyred

What kind of driver doesn't need a licence?
A screwdriver

What do you call a vicar on a motorbike?
Rev

When is a car not a car?
When it turns into a road

What is the laziest part of a car?
The wheels, because they're always tyred

What has wheels and goes "hic, hic, hic"?
A hiccup truck

What did the jack say to the car?
"Can I give you a lift?"

What vegetable do you not want in a boat?
A leek

Why isn't it safe to sleep on trains?
Because they run over sleepers

What did the traffic light say to the car?
"Close your eyes, I'm changing."

How do locomotives hear?
Through the engine-ears

What do you call a man with a speedometer on his head?
Miles

What do you call a woman with a sinking ship on her head?
Mandy Lifeboats

Knock, knock
Who's there?
Cargo
Cargo who?
Cargo vroom vroom

Knock, knock
Who's there?
Tank
Tank who?
You're welcome

Why did the man call his car Baby?
Because it always went with a rattle

What do you call a man with a car on his head?
Jack

First bird: "Wow, look how fast those planes fly."
Second bird: "You'd fly that fast too if your bum was on fire!"

What were Batman and Robin called after they got run over by a bus?
Flatman and Ribbon

"What made you want to do a parachute jump?"
"The plane was on fire."

"I swam 10,000 meters in five seconds."
"How did you do that?"
"I went over a waterfall."

What runs all day but is never out of breath?
A train

"My car's got a puncture."
"I told you to watch out for the fork in the road."

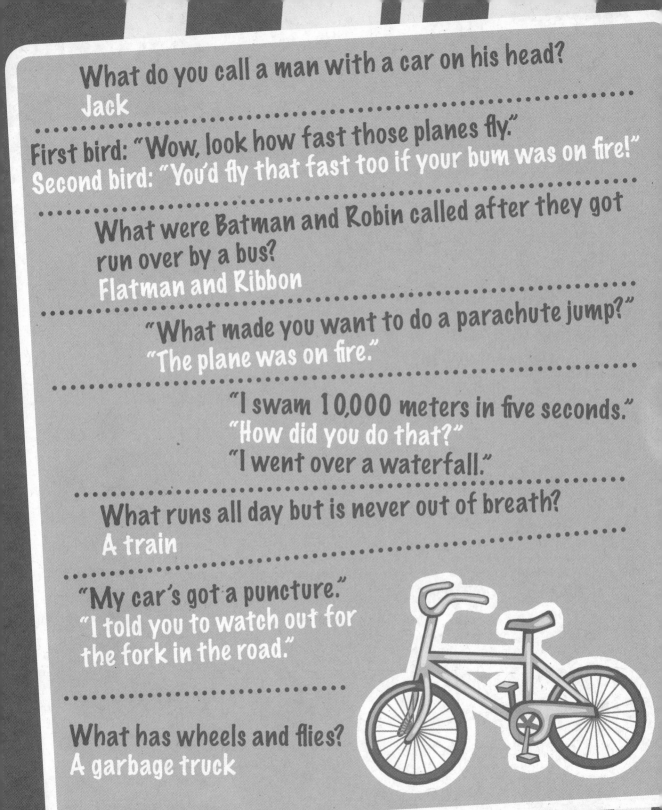

What has wheels and flies?
A garbage truck

What do you do with old bikes?
Re-cycle them

What did the driver say to the hitchhiking kangaroo?
"Hop in."

What do you call a German in a motorcycle hat?
Helmut

What did the traffic warden say to the frog that was parked illegally?
"Hop it or I'll have you toad away."

What are cheeky, pink and wear sneakers?
Jogging bottoms

Why did the ram crash his car?
He didn't see the ewe turn

Girl: "My dad drives like lightning"
Boy: "You mean he drives fast?"
Girl: "No, he hits trees."

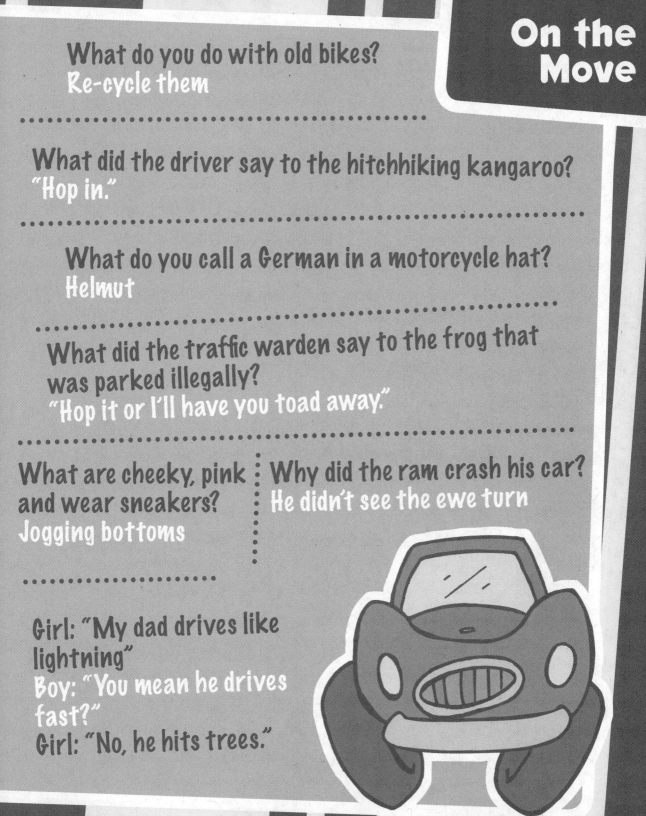

What do old car wheels do?
Re-tyre

What do you call a bike that keeps hurting people?
A vicious cycle

What do you call a ejector seat in a helicopter?
A bad idea

What do you call a traffic warden who never writes any tickets?
A terrific warden

What do you call a blonde police officer?
A fair cop

What do you call the history of a car?
An autobiography

What does a train driver wear on his feet?
Platform shoes

Why are hairdressers good drivers?
They know all the short cuts

How do you top a car?
Tep on the brake, tupid

Parachute for sale, no strings attached

Why are train drivers always worried?
Because their jobs are on the line

What do you call a lorry
full of feet?
A toe truck

What do you call a car that
acts in movies?
Harrison Ford

What's a ten-letter word that starts with gas?
Automobile

If a whole country drove pink cars what would it be?
A pink car-nation

Where do cars go swimming?
In a car pool

Why did the beggar get thrown off the ship?
Because beggars can't be cruisers

What did the frog do when his car broke down?
He got toad

What happened to the wooden car?
It wooden go

Why can't a bicycle stand up by itself?
Because it's two tyred

Who can hold up a bus with one hand?
A police officer

Why couldn't G-Unit use the bus?
They only had 50 Cent

What do you call a flying policeman?
A helicopper

"I've never flown before," said the nervous old lady to the pilot. "You will bring me down safely won't you?"
"Well, I've never left anyone up there yet!"

What do you call a musical automobile?
A cartoon

What type of car does an electrician drive?
A volts-wagon

Why do cars smell?
Because they're full of gas

What kind of lights did Noah have on the ark?
Flood lights

What did the tornado say to the car? "Do you want to go for a spin?"

What is the most tired part of a car? The exhaust pipe

What's worse than raining cats and dogs? Hailing taxis

What do cars, trees and elephants all have in common? Trunks

What did the bug say when it hit the windshield? "I don't have the guts to do that again."

What did the doctor give the sick car? A fuel injection

What does a train do with its food?
Choo-choo

What kind of vehicles do Disney characters drive?
Minnie-vans

Which American state is the best for driving?
Rhode island

What did Geronimo say when he jumped out the plane?
"Meeeeeeeeee!"

What kind of motorbike can cook eggs?
A scrambler

What do you call a toy railway?
A play station

How long did it take the shoe to cross the road?
The same time it took the person

What do you call a woman with a boat on her head?
Maude

What do you get if you put herbs in your computer?
A thyme machine

Why did the computer go crazy?
Because it had a screw loose

Why did the robot get a manicure?
He had rusty nails

Why shouldn't you give your mouse cheese?
It makes a real mess of your computer

Why don't elephants use computers?
Because they're afraid of the mouse

Why did the computer sneeze?
It had a virus

What did the computer have for lunch?
A byte to eat

Why was the computer so tired?
It had a hard drive

Why don't Vikings send email?
They prefer to use Norse code

Man: "I've just pushed a piece of bacon into my computer"
Helpline: "Has the computer stopped working?"
Man: "No, but there's a lot of crackling."

How do you stop your laptop batteries running out?
Hide their sneakers

What do you get if you cross a computer with a hamburger?
A Big Mac

What did one keyboard say to the other keyboard?
You're not my type

What did the mouse say to the webcam?
"Cheese"

Why didn't the idiot get any email?
Because the e-dog kept chasing the e-postman

Who sits on Cinderella's keyboard?
Buttons

How do runners send email?
On the sprinter-net

DISK
FILE

How do you get rid of internettles?
Always weed your email

How can you tell when a robot is mad?
He goes screwy

Did the robot have any brothers?
No but he had plenty of tran-sisters

Why didn't the mouse cross the road?
The cord wasn't long enough

How did the computer thief get out of jail?
He pressed the escape key

Why did the computer wear glasses?
To improve its web sight

Why did the computer cross the road?
Because the chicken programmed it to

Why did the spider cross the information super highway?
To get to her website

What do computer operators eat for lunch?
Micro-chips

What did the robot eat for a light snack?
A 100-watt bulb

What did the mother robot say to her children?
Look before you bleep

What do you get if you cross a laptop and a warlock?
A computer wizard

Why didn't the girl mouse like the boy mouse?
They just didn't click

What do rabbits put in their computers?
Hoppy discs

What do you get if you cross a PC and an elephant?
A computer with a really big memory

What do you get if you cross a computer with a rhino?
A broken desk

What do you get if you cross a telephone with some trousers?
Bell bottoms

What do you get if you cross a computer virus and a vampire?
A nasty byte

What did the light bulb say to its mother?
"I love you watts and watts."

Why did the computer squeak?
Someone trod on its mouse

How do you find monsters on the internet?
Use a lurch engine

How do you know if an idiot's been using the computer?
There's correction fluid on the screen

What do you put in a www-indows?
Net curtains

Where do computers take their sick pets?
To the intervet

What happens if you get a gigabyte?
It megahertz

Why are beavers always on the internet?
They never log off

Why did the germ cross
the microscope?
To get to the other slide

What did the big cell phone say to the little cell phone?
"You're too small to be engaged."

What do you call it
when you've been bitten
by a big computer?
A megabyte

What do you get if you
cross a computer with
a million mosquitos?
A gigabyte

Why was the computer good at golf?
Because it had a hard drive

Why was the computer cold?
It forgot to close its windows

Why was the computer injured?
It had a slipped disc

What kind of music do computers like?
Disc-o

Why was the fisherman mad at the computer?
Because he wasn't getting any bytes

What part of the computer was the alien's favorite?
The space bar

How do you catch a computer fish?
Online or in the net

What was the baby computer's first word?
Data

What do you call a campground for spiders?
A website

What do you call a man with a computer on his head?
CD Ron

What do you call a woman with a computerized piano on the side of her head?
Cynthia

What do you call a woman with a computerized piano on top of her head?
Hyacinth

Why did the ant elope?
Nobody gnu

What do you call an ant
with five pairs of eyes?
Ant-ten-eye

What do you call an ant that lives alone?
Independ-ant

Where do stupid ants live?
Ant-twerp

How do you cure a poisoned ant?
Give him the ant-idote

There were two snakes in the desert
One asked the other, "What's 74 minus 23?"
"How should I know?" replied the second snake
"I'm an adder."

Why do bees have sticky hair?
Because of the honeycombs

Why wasn't the butterfly allowed to the dance?
Because it was a moth ball

What's a bee's favorite flower?
Bee-gonia

If bees make honey, what do wasps make?
Wasp-berry jam

A vampire bat returned to his cave one night covered in fresh blood. All the other bats were hungry and asked him where he had got it from. At first he wouldn't tell them, but they kept on pestering him until finally he gave in and said he would show them.

"Follow me," he said and flew out of the cave with hundreds of bats close behind him. Over the mountains they went, down into the valley and across the river, until they arrived at a vast forest full of trees.

"Now," said the first bat to the group, "you see that tree over there?"

"Yes, yes," they all cried excitedly

"Well, I didn't," said the bat

What do you call a baby ant?
An inf-ant

What's black and yellow and buzzes at 35,000 feet?
A bee in a plane

What's worse than finding a worm in your apple?
Finding half a worm in your apple

What do you get if you cross a centipede and a chicken?
Enough drumsticks to feed an army

How can you tell if a snake is a baby snake?
It has a rattle

Why are glow worms good creatures to put in a heavy bag?
They lighten the load

What animal is good at cricket?
A bat

First bat: "Do you fancy going out for a bite?"
Second bat: "No, I think I'll just hang around."

What's even better than a talking dog?
A spelling bee

What do you call a bee that can't make up its mind?
A may-bee

What do you call a beetle in a spacesuit?
Bug Lightyear

What do you call a nervous insect?
A jitterbug

What kind of frog has horns?
A bull frog

What's the definition of a caterpillar?
A worm in a fur coat

What lies on the ground, 100 feet up in the air and smells?
A dead centipede

Why did the flea get the sack from the flea circus?
He wasn't up to scratch

Did you hear about the angry flea?
He was hopping mad

What do you call a positive flea?
A hop-timist

What did the bus driver say to the frog?
Hop on

What happened to the frog that parked his car illegally?
He was toad away

Why was the frog crying?
He was un-hoppy

Where do frogs keep their coats?
In the croak-room

How do you start an insect race?
"One, two, flea, go!"

What's another name for an Australian gecko?
The Lizard of Oz

What do you call a crane fly with a gun?
Baddy long legs

What goes buzz-dash-dash, buzz-dot-dot?
A morse-quito

Why couldn't the viper viper nose?
Because the adder adder handkerchief

What do venomous snakes have?
Poison-ality

What says dot-dot-croak, dash-dash-croak?
Morse toad

What do you call a bee that's always moaning?
A grumble bee

What do snakes have on their bathroom walls?
Rep-tiles

What is a skunk's favorite game?
Ping pong

How many skunks does it take to change a light bulb?
A phew

How did the skunk ring his best friend?
On his smell-ular phone

What do you call a mad flea?
A loony tic

What do you call a retired fly?
A flew

What did the glow worm say when he left the party?
Bye, I'm glowing now

What do you call fighting bees?
Rumble bees

Why did the dad caterpillar run out of money?
He had to buy the kids new shoes

What's long and green and goes "hith"?
A snake with a lisp

Why don't anteaters get sick?
Because they are full of antibodies

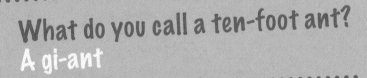

What do you call a ten-foot ant?
A gi-ant

Where do ants like to go on holiday?
Ant-igua

What do you call an ant that skips school?
A tru-ant

What did the teacher say
to the naughty bee?
"Will you beehive!"

Why do bees hum?
Because they can't
remember the words

What's green and dangerous?
A caterpillar with a machine gun

What do frogs drink?
Croak-a-Cola

What is an insect's favorite sport?
Cricket

What was the snake's favorite subject at school?
Hiss-tory

What insect runs away from everything?
A flea

What do frogs order at the drive thru?
French flies and diet croak

Why was the centipede dropped from the soccer team?
He took too long putting his boots on

What is the definition of a slug?
A snail with a housing problem

There were two snakes basking on a rock. One turned to the other and asked, "Are we the type of snakes that coil around our prey and crush it to death, or are we the kind that bite it and poison it with our venom?"
"Why do you ask?" said the second snake
"Because I just bit my lip."

How do you stop a skunk from smelling?
Hold its nose

How many legs does an ant have?
Two, the same as an uncle

What happened when the American stoats got married?
They became the united stoats of America

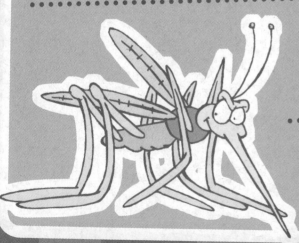

What goes buzzzz, zzzzzub, buzzzz, zzzzub?
A bee in a yoyo

Where do bees go to catch public transport?
The buzz stop

What did the frog say to the toad?
"Warts new?"

What do you get if you cross a galaxy with a toad?
Star Warts

How do snails fight?
They slug it out

Knock, knock
Who's there?
Amos
Amos who?
Amos-quito is trying to bite me. Please let me in

What did one hot bee say to the other?
"Swarm."

What did the bee say to the flower?
"Hello honey."

Where do tadpoles change?
In the croakroom

What should you do if there is a tarantula in your bed?
Sleep somewhere else

Did you hear the joke about the skunk?
It stinks

What type of animal isn't truthful?
An am-fib-ian

Which letter of the alphabet is also an insect?
B

Why did the snail cross the road?
I don't know it hasn't got there yet

What did one bee say to the other?
It's none of your buzzness

What does a bumble bee sit on?
His bee-hind

Did you hear about the argumentative skunk?
It liked to cause a stink

What did the judge say when he sentenced the skunk?
"Odor in court."

What do you call a flying skunk?
A smellicopter

What happened to the skunk that couldn't swim?
He stank

Why can't skunks keep secrets?
Because people are always getting wind of them

What was the skunk's favorite part of school?
Show and smell

What's a skunk's philosophy on life?
Eat, stink and be merry

How do skunks avoid danger?
By using their in-stinks and common scents

What sort of snake will tell on you?
A grass snake

What did the bees do in their new hive?
They had a hive-swarming party

What do you give a sick snake?
Asp-rin

What do frogs drink at bed time?
Croako

Why are male ants better at swimming than female ants?
Because they're boy-ant

Why did the frog cross the road?
To see what was hoppening on the other side

What was the frog's favorite ballet?
Swamp Lake

Which insect can tell your fortune?
A gypsy moth

What is a caterpillar afraid of?
A dogerpillar

Which hand would you use to grab a venomous snake?
Someone else's

Why didn't the broken skunk smell?
It was out of odor

Why did the snake become a priest?
He got the coiling

Why do bees buzz?
Because they can't whistle

Who was the bee's favorite artist?
Pablo Bee-casso

What tastes sweet and has big sharp teeth?
A chocodile

What do you get if you cross a serpent and a trombone?
A snake in the brass

What do you call lots of panicking snakes?
Mass hiiisssss-teria

What do you call a girl with bees on her head?
Abbey Hive

What do you call a lady worm?
A worman

Why did the termite eat the sofa and chairs?
He had a suite tooth

Why did the sunbathing frog go to the doctors?
He had heat croak

How much did the American pay for the skunk?
One scent

Why was the mother flea sad?
All her children had gone to the dogs

What did the snake say when the lizard asked it for the time?
"Don't asp me."

How do you make a moth ball?
Hit it on the nose

What do bees chew?
Bumble gum

What's yellow, black and covered in berries?
A bramble bee

What can fly, has six legs, speaks Norwegian and bites?
A Norse-quito

Why was 2004 a good year for frogs?
It was a leap year

Did you hear about the pregnant snake?
She gave birth to a bouncing baby boa

What do you call a homeless snail?
A slug

What's the difference between a fly and a monster?
Quite a lot really

What game do dinosaurs play with ants?
Squash

What do you get if you cross a snail with Dracula?
The slowest vampire in the world

What did the slug say to the other slug that hit him and ran off?
I'll get you next slime

What do you get if you cross a glow worm with a pint of beer?
Light ale

What's white, wriggly and dangerous?
A maggot with a bad attitude

Why do worms taste like chewing gum?
Because they're Wrigleys

Why did the boa constrictors date?
They had a crush on each other

Why are snakes hard to fool?
They don't have any legs to pull

What do you call a python with the gift of the gab?
A snake charmer

What is a snake's favorite dance?
The mamba

What do you get if you cross two snakes with magic spells?
Addercadabra and abradacobra

What do you do if you find a black mamba in your toilet?
Wait until it's finished

What did one frog say to the other?
Time's fun when you having flies

Two boy silkworms pursued a luscious girl silkworm.
They ended up in a tie

What do fireflies eat?
Light snacks

Who wrote 'Keeping Snakes'?
Sir Pent

Who wrote 'How To Keep Amphibians'?
Ivor Toad

What type of shoes do frogs wear?
Open toad sandals

Knock, knock
Who's there?
Adder
Adder who?
Adder you get in here?

Who wrote 'How To
Catch Wriggly Bugs'?
Tina Worms

Why did the clock scratch?
It had ticks

How do fleas travel?
They itch-hike

What do you get if you cross a snake with a pastry?
A pie-thon

Did you hear about the two frogs that tried to kiss in the fog?
They mist

What is a spider's favorite food?
Corn on the cob-web

Why don't bats live alone?
They like to hang around with their friends

What is smaller than an ant's mouth?
An ant's dinner

What's green and loud?
A froghorn

Why shouldn't you step on a frog?
Because you'll make him hopping mad

Where do ghosts go on vacation?
The Dead Sea

Where else do ghosts go on vacation?
Lake Eerie

What do you call a nerdy vampire?
Dorkula

Did you hear about the man who quit his job as an undertaker?
He thought it was a dead-end job

What kind of road did the ghost live on?
A dead end

What do you call a ghost policeman?
A chief in-spectre

A ghost walked into a bar and asked the barman for a double whiskey.
The barman replied, "Sorry, we don't serve spirits."

What did the werewolf eat after he had a tooth out?
The dentist

Why don't vampires like arguing?
Because they don't want to get cross

In what way are vampires artistic?
They're good at drawing blood

What delivers monster babies?
The Frankenstork

Where does a witch keep her purse?
In her hag bag

How does a vampire enter his house?
Through the bat flap

Witch: "Doctor, doctor, I don't feel very well."
Doctor: "Stay in bed for a spell."

What do little monsters take to bed?
Deady bears

Why did the boy take a clock
and a chick out on Halloween?
Because it was tick or tweet

What's a vampire's favorite drink?
A Bloody Mary

Where do vampires keep their money?
At the blood bank

Why didn't the skeleton go to the party?
He had no body to go with

Where do vampires go fishing?
In the blood stream

Boy: "What has 20 legs, 12 eyes and red and green fur?"
Girl: "I don't know."
Boy: "I don't know either, but you've got one crawling up your leg."

What sort of wine do skeletons like?
One with plenty of body

What do ghouls eat for breakfast?
Dreaded wheat

How does a witch feel on long journeys?
Broom-sick

What happened to the witch who lost her temper with her broomstick?
She flew off the handle

Why do witches only ride their broomsticks after dark?
That's the time to go to sweep

What pasta do ghosts like best?
Spook-etti

What dessert do ghosts like best?
Boo-berry pie

What does Dracula take when he has a cold?
Coffin medicine

First ghost: "You look tired."
Second ghost: "Yes, I'm dead on my feet."

What do ghosts have on their sandwiches?
Boo-loney

Why didn't the vampire have any friends?
He was a pain in the neck

What's Dracula's favorite sport?
Bat-minton

What has webbed feet and fangs?
Count Duckula

What was the demon's favorite sitcom?
Fiends

Why was the graveyard so noisy?
Because of all the coffin

What do you call an ugly hag who stops cars with her thumb?
A witch-hiker

What do ghost school children write their homework in?
Exorcise books

Why did the vampire go to hospital?
To have his ghoul-stones removed

Man: "Who was that at the door?"
Woman: "The invisible man."
Man: "Tell him I can't see him."

What happened to the hag who fell in poison ivy?
She was an itchy witchy

Why do vampires drink blood?
Cola makes them burp

Doctor Jekyll has created a medicine.
One sip and you're a new man

What do monsters do when they have sore throats?
Gargoyle

What kind of monster fits on the end of your finger?
A bogeyman

What did Quasimodo say when the teacher asked him a question?
"I have a hunch..."

Knock, knock
Who's there?
Turner
Turner who?
Turner round slowly, there's a monster behind you

Knock, knock
Who's there?
Oliver
Oliver who?
Oliver lone and I'm scared of monsters

What do you get if you cross a plum with a monster?
A purple people eater

What do you call a friendly monster?
A failure

Why was the operating theater haunted?
It was full of surgical spirits

Why did the ghost go to the theater?
To watch the phanto-mime

What is a baby ghost's favorite bedtime story?
Ghoul-dilocks

What's large, green and sits in the corner and cries?
The incredible sulk

Why did the zombie stay in bed?
He felt rotten

What do devil's drink?
Demonade

What is monster's favorite cheese?
Monster-ella

What do you get if you cross a monster with a skunk?
Stinkenstein

Why don't ghosts like rain?
It dampens their spirits

What do you call a witch at the beach?
A sand-witch

Why don't mummies have any friends?
They're too wrapped up in themselves

What do you call a monster at a disco?
The boogie-man

What is a vampire's favorite fruit?
Neck-terines

What was the ghost's
favorite nursery rhyme?
Little Boo Peep

Why did Doctor Jekyll cross the road?
To get to the other Hyde

· ·

Who did the ghost take to the movies?
His ghoul-friend

· ·

Why are ghosts bad liars?
You can see right through them

What did the sad ghost say?
"Boo hoo."

· ·

Why do skeletons play pianos?
Because they don't have any organs

· ·

What did the monster read in the newspaper?
His horror-scope

· ·

What game do ghosts like playing?
Hide and shriek

· ·

How do you make a skeleton laugh?
Tickle his funny bone

Knock, knock
Who's there?
Witches
Witches who?
Witches the way home?

Where would you find a giant snail?
On the end of his finger

What do you call a witch who drives badly?
A road hag

What's black and has eight wheels?
A witch on roller skates

How do witches tell the time?
They wear witch watches

What did the hippy vampire say?
"Ghoul, man, real ghoul."

What do you call a ghost's mother?
Transparent

How do you make a monster stew?
Keep him waiting for three hours

What happened when the vampire went mad?
He went a little batty

Why do devils and ghosts get on so well?
Because demons are a ghoul's best friend

What did the vampire say to the werewolf?
"You look like you're going to the dogs."

Why did the witch call hotel reception?
She wanted broom service

What goes ha ha ha bonk?
A zombie laughing his head off

Why don't mummies like to rest?
They're afraid to unwind

Who won the vampire race?
No one, it was neck and neck

Where do Chinese vampires live?
Fang-hai

Why are vampires polite?
They always say fangs

What is Dracula's favorite ice-cream?
Vein-illa

What do you get if you cross
Dracula and Sir Lancelot?
A bite in shining armor

What is a vampire's favorite fruit?
Blood oranges

What's pink and has a curly
tail and fangs?
A ham-pire

What's white, fluffy
and hates garlic?
A lamb-pire

What do you call an unmarried vampire?
A bat-chelor

Why was Doctor Frankenstein never lonely?
He was good at making friends

Where do zombies go on cruises?
The Dead-iterranean

What do you call a clever monster?
Frank Einstein

Why did the vampire go to the blood bank?
To make a withdrawal

How do skeletons call their friends?
On the tele-bone

What is a vampire's favorite soup?
Scream of tomato

What did the witch doctor
say to the tribeswoman?
Voodoo like to dance?

What airline do monsters fly on?
British Scare-ways

Which ghost scared James Bond?
Ghoul-dfinger

How do you address a monster?
Very politely

What is a monster's favorite aftershave?
Brute

Who wrote a book called
'The Haunted House'?
Hugo First

Knock, knock
Who's there?
Jacqueline
Jacqueline who?
Jacqueline Hyde

Knock, knock
Who's there?
Avon
Avon who?
Avon to drink your blood

What did the
monster get when
he fell through the
window?
A pane

What is the first thing
you should put into a
haunted house?
Someone else

What does a vampire get
when he drinks too much?
A fangover

Did you hear about the musical mummy?
He was in a rock bandage

Did you hear about the werewolf who dropped his trousers?
It was a full moon

How do you get rid of a vampire?
Ask him if he'd like garlic mushrooms with his steak

How did the skeleton boy get to school?
On the skull bus

Why did the werewolf eat the jogger?
He liked fast food

What did the short-sighted ghost wear?
Spectre-ghouls

How do vampires wash?
In a blood bath

What do you call a vampire with no teeth?
Pointless

What do you call a vampire you can dip in your tea?
Count Dunkula

What do you call a lost hairy man-dog?
A where-am-I wolf

What view did the mummy get from the top of the pyramids?
As pharaoh the eye can see

Where do you go to get a Dracula costume?
Vamp-hire

What did Frankenstein do when the monster's head fell off?
He made a bolt for it

What did the ghost call his teddy bear?
Winnie the ooooooohhhhhhhh

How do vampires start a duel?
Drac to Drac

What do you call a lazy skeleton?
Bone idle

What do zombies put on their roast beef?
Grave-y

What do you get if you cross a vampire with a raincoat?
Macula

Why did Ghoul-dilocks go to Egypt?
She wanted to see the mummy bear

What sort of jokes are a werewolf's favorite?
Howlers

Why did the shy werewolf hide in the wardrobe every full moon?
He didn't like anyone to see him changing

What does it say on the mummy's garage door?
Toot and come in

Why was the mummy tense?
He had been wound up

Where do ghouls mail their letters?
In the ghost box

Who delivers them?
The ghostman

How do you grow a werewolf?
Use plenty of fur-tilizer

Who travels on haunted airways?
Air ghostesses and lots of high spirits

What do you call a fat mummy?
Two-ton Carmen

What type of horses do ghosts ride?
Night-mares

What do sea monsters eat?
Fish and ships

What do baby sea
monsters play with?
Doll-phins

What did the monster say
when he saw the crowded
swimming pool?
"Oh look, soup!"

What do you call a
stupid vampire?
A clot

Did the ghost enjoy the party?
Yes he had a wail of a time

How did the ghost begin his letter?
"Tomb it may concern."

Which sea monster swims in his under wear?
The Loch Vest Monster

Which sea monster is untidy?
The Loch Mess Monster

What do you call a positive sea monster?
The Loch Yes Monster

Why are vampires so stupid?
Because blood is thicker than water

What is a monster's favorite flavor snack?
Squeeze and bunion

Where does Dracula go on vacation?
Holiday vamp

What vegetables do monsters eat with their Christmas dinner?
Boy sprouts

Where do ghouls post their letters?
At the ghost office

How do you make a witch itch?
Take away the w

What kind of tests do witches take?
Hex-aminations

What do monsters call humans?
Dinner

How many witches does it take to change a light bulb?
Into what?

What do you say to a three-headed monster?
"Hello hello hello."

Where do little ghosts learn to say "boo"?
At noisery school

What do you call serious rocks?
Grave stones

What does a ghost have for breakfast?
Rice Creepies

What sort of mail do ghosts get?
Chain letters

Why was the zombie grumpy?
He woke up too early in the mourning

What did the ghoul send
when he was on holiday?
Ghostcards

What did he write on it?
"Witch you were here."

Why wasn't the
gravedigger working?
He was on his coffin break

What happened when the dog buried the skeleton's bone?
He didn't have a leg to stand on

Why did the ghoul take the zombie for a drive?
Because he was a car-case

What do zombies eat with bread and cheese?
Pickled organs

Why do ghosts go to the sales?
They like bargain haunting

What puzzles do vampires like?
Crypt-ic crosswords

Why did the witch put her wand in the oven?
She wanted a hot spell

What do you call a wizard on a broomstick?
A flying sorcerer

Why did the vampire like watching sport?
He was a football fang

Why did the ghost go into hospital?
To get his ghoul stones removed

What do you get if you cross a vampire with a plumber?
A drain in the neck

What is a vampire's favorite sport?
Drac racing

Why did the vampire stay up so late?
He was studying for his blood test

Where does Dracula get his pencils?
Pencil-vania

Where do vampire fish live?
In the blood stream

Why didn't the servant return when Dracula sent him to get a paper?
He was out for the Count

How do you talk to a monster?
Use big words

Why can't vampires write poetry?
They go from bat to verse

First monster: "Oh dear am I late for dinner?"
Second monster: "Yes, everybody's already been eaten."

What did the vampire say when he saw the sleeping lady?
"Breakfast in bed."

How do warty witches keep their hair out of place?
With scare spray!

Who did Dracula have a crush on?
The girl necks door

Why did the stupid monster put his hands over his ears?
He was trying to hold on to a thought

Why did the vampire use a red pencil?
So that he could draw blood

What did the zombie's friend say when he introduced him to his girlfriend?
"Oh my goodness where did you dig her up?"

Why did the werewolf bring toilet paper to the party?
Because he was a party pooper

What kind of fur do you get from a vampire?
As fur away as possible

Where do American vampires work?
The Vampire State Building

What do you call a 15-foot monster?
Shorty

Why was the vampire an embarrassment to his father?
He fainted at the sight of blood

How come the monster didn't get a single hair on his head wet when he went out in the rain?
He didn't have a head

How do you make a monster's eyes light up?
Shine a torch in his ears

What do you do when a monster throws a hand grenade at you?
Pull out the pin and throw it back

How does a monster clean his house?
With a victim cleaner

What do you call a dream where you are being attacked by vampires?
A bitemare

What do you call the spot in the middle of the graveyard?
Dead center

Why was the ghost arrested?
He didn't have a haunting licence

What happened to the vampires who fell in love?
They loved in vein

What do you call a ghostly teddy bear?
Haun-ted

How was the bicycle ghost proof?
It didn't have any spooks

How do you tell a friendly monster from an unfriendly one?
If he's friendly you'll be able to talk about it later

Why did the monster cross the road?
He wanted to know what it was like being a chicken

When do banshees wail?
On moanday night

What do you give a monster with big feet?
Big shoes

First monster: "I was in the zoo last week."
Second monster: "Really which cage were you in?"

Man: "The police are looking for a monster with one eye."
Woman: "Why don't they use both their eyes?"

What happened when the monster sent his picture to the lonely hearts agency?
They sent it back saying they weren't that lonely

How do you keep a stupid ugly monster in suspense?
I'll tell you tomorrow

First zombie: "That beautiful creature just rolled her eyes at me."
Second zombie: "Well roll them back, she might need them."

What ghoul has the best hearing?
The eeriest

What did the skeleton say to his girlfriend?
"I love every bone in your body."

What is big, hairy and scary and jumps up and down?
A monster on a pogo stick

What do you get if you cross a pen with a big green monster?
The ink-redible hulk

What happened to the monster that ate too much uranium?
He got atomic-ache

Who do zombie cowboys fight?
Deadskins

What do you call zombies in a belfry?
Dead ringers

What does Frankenstein's monster call a screwdriver?
Daddy

Who wrote 'The Angry Werewolf'?
Claudia Armoff

Why did Dracula go to the dentist?
He had fang decay

Why did Dracula have fang decay?
He ate too many fang-cy cakes

What does the postman deliver to Dracula?
Fang mail

A new fang-led device

What did the vampire call his daughter?
Bloody Mary

What do you call a hairy beast with clothes on?
A wear wolf

What do you call a hairy beast in a river?
A weir wolf

Why didn't the skeleton cross the road?
He didn't have the guts

What did the ghost eat at the birthday party?
I scream

Why didn't the monster make the team?
Because he threw like a ghoul

What did the witch's broom do when it was tired?
It went to sweep

What is Dracula's favorite movie?
The Vampire Strikes Back

What do witches put in their hair?
Scare-spray

Where do ghosts go when they're sick?
To the witch doctor

Why do vampires use mouthwash?
Because they have bat breath

What did the cool ghost say to the other cool ghost?
"Get a life, dude."

What was the ghost's favorite song?
Ghouls Just Wanna Have Fun

Which monster plays jokes on Halloween?
Prank-enstein

What did the skeleton buy at the butchers?
Spare ribs

What do you call a skeleton that won't get out of bed?
Lazy bones

What do vampires play poker for?
High stakes

What was the vampire's favorite holiday?
Fangs giving

What type of music do mummies like?
Wrap music

Why can't skeletons sing in church?
They don't have any organs

What do you call a ghost that puts out fires?
A fire frighter

What did the papa ghost say to the baby ghost?
Fasten your sheet belt

What did Tutankhamen say when he was scared?
"I want my mummy."

What does a dentist call x-rays?
Tooth pics

"Doctor, doctor, I keep thinking I'm a doctor-eating monster."
"That's a shame. I'm a dentist."

"Doctor, doctor, I think I'm an apple."
"We must get to the core of this."

Did you hear about the dentist who became a brain surgeon?
His drill slipped

"Doctor, doctor, I keep seeing an insect walking around in circles."
"Don't worry, it's just a bug that's going around."

"Doctor, doctor, I'm nervous. This is the first brain operation for me."
"Don't worry, it's the first for me, too."

"Doctor, doctor, I keep thinking I'm invisible."
"Who said that?"

"Doctor, doctor, I keep thinking I'm a cat."
"How long have you felt like this?"
"Since I was a kitten."

"Doctor, doctor, I keep thinking I'm a mosquito."
"Go away, sucker."

Knock, knock
Who's there?
Kenya
Kenya who?
Kenya fix my broken leg?

"Doctor, doctor, will these pills really cure me?"
"Well, no one else I gave them to has ever come back."

"Doctor, doctor, I'm at death's door."
"Don't worry, an operation will pull you through."

"Doctor, doctor, I've got a little stye."
"You had better buy a little pig then."

What happens when a psychiatrist tells you that you're schizophrenic?
He charges you double

"Doctor, doctor, I feel like a tennis racquet."
"You must be highly strung."

"Doctor, doctor, I keep thinking I'm a yo-yo."
"How do you feel?"
"Up and down."

"Doctor, doctor, I feel run down."
"Look both ways before crossing the road next time."

"Doctor, doctor, my tummy hurts."
"Stop your belly-aching."

"Doctor, doctor, I feel like a hamster."
"Then go see a vet."

"Doctor, doctor, I feel like a piano"
"Hold on, I'll take some notes."

"Doctor, doctor, I've swallowed a roll of film."
"Let's wait and see what develops."

When do doctors get angry?
When they run out of patients

Why did the nurse creep past the medicine cabinet?
She didn't want to wake the sleeping tablets

Why is a psychiatrist like a squirrel?
They're both surrounded by nuts

"Doctor, doctor, can you help me out?"
"Yes sir, the door's over there."

"Doctor, doctor, everyone thinks I'm a liar."
"I don't believe you."

"Doctor, doctor, I feel like a window."
"Where's the pane?"

What time should you go to the dentist?
Tooth-hurty.

"Doctor, doctor, I swallowed a bone."
"Are you choking?"
"No, I'm telling the truth."

"Doctor, doctor, I think I'm suffering from déjà vu."
"Didn't I see you yesterday?"

"Doctor, doctor, I keep thinking I'm a sheep."
"How do you feel?"
"Baaaad."

"Doctor, doctor, I feel like a
deck of cards."
"I'll deal with you later."

"Doctor, doctor, I'm boiling."
"Simmer down."

....

"Doctor, doctor, when I press here my finger hurts. And here. And here. What do you think is wrong with me?"
"Your finger's broken."

....

"Doctor, doctor, I keep thinking I'm a vampire."
"Necks please."

....

"Doctor, doctor, I think I'm a caterpillar."
"Don't worry, you'll soon change."

....

"Doctor, doctor, I keep forgetting things."
"When did this start?"
"When did what start?"

....

"Doctor, doctor, I think I'm a moth."
"Get out of the way, you're in my light."

....

"Doctor, doctor, I feel like a dog."
"Sit."

....

"Doctor, doctor,
I feel like a pin."
"I see your point."

"Doctor, doctor, I think I'm a drill."
"How boring for you."

"Doctor, doctor, I've got strawberries growing out of my head."
"Here's some cream for them."

"Doctor, doctor, I keep thinking I'm a snowman."
"Stay cool."

Girl: "I'd love to be an actress."
Boy: "Break a leg, then."
Girl: "Why?"
Boy: "Because then you'd be in a cast for weeks."

"Doctor, doctor, my right leg hurts."
"I expect it's just old age."
"But my left leg doesn't hurt and it's just as old as my right one."

Knock, knock
Who's there?
Doctor
Doctor who?
No Doctor Jones – you called me because you have flu.

Why did the angel go to the doctors?
She thought she had harp faliure

What is faster hot or cold?
Hot – you can catch a cold

"Doctor, Doctor I snore so loud I keep myself awake."
Sleep in another room then!

"Doctor, doctor, I feel like a pair of scissors."
"Well cut that out to start with."

"Doctor, doctor, I feel like a cash register."
"Come back later and tell me if there's any change."

"Doctor, doctor, I keep seeing red and green spots."
"Have you seen an optician?"
"No, just spots."

"Doctor, doctor, I've got carrots in my ears."
"How did that happen?"
"I don't know, I planted potatoes."

"Doctor, doctor, I've broken
my leg what shall I do?"
"Limp."

"Doctor, doctor, what are my
chances of losing weight?"
"Slim."

How many psychiatrists does it take to change a light bulb?
Only one, but the light bulb has to really want to change

What is a chiropodist's favorite song?
There's No Business Like Toe Business

Why did the biscuit go to the doctors?
It was feeling crummy

"Doctor, doctor, I think I've got Delhi belly."
"I expect it's just India-gestion."

What do surgeons do with their mistakes?
Bury them

Does an apple a day keep the doctor away?
It does if your aim's good enough

What do you get if someone hits you on the head with an axe?
A splitting headache

AMBULANCE

"Doctor, doctor, I think I'm a dog."
"How do you feel?"
"Ruff."

Knock, knock
Who's there?
Ivan
Ivan who?
Ivan nasty disease,
don't come too close

What do you call a woman with only one tooth?
Peg

How do you make a Venetian blind?
Stick you finger in his eye

"Doctor, doctor, my sister thinks she's an elevator."
"Tell her to come and see me."
"I can't, she doesn't stop at this floor."

An apple a day keeps the doctor away, but
an onion a day keeps everyone away

Why did the carpenter
go to the doctor?
He had a saw hand

What is the cure
for dandruff?
Baldness

What was the name of the Scottish dentist?
Phil McCavity

Doctor: "Stick your tongue out and say 'aaaarrrgh'."
Patient: "Aaaarrrgh."
Doctor: "Yuck, you're not going to put that back in your mouth are you?"

What two letters are bad for your teeth?
D-K

"Doctor, doctor, my belly is really fat."
"I think you should diet."
"What color?"

"Doctor, doctor, I burned myself making pancakes."
"How waffle."

"Doctor, doctor, people keep telling me I'm a wheelbarrow."
"Don't let them push you around."

"Doctor, doctor, how can I make my cough better?"
"Keep practicing."

Why did the doctor put the patient under the bed?
He thought she was a little potty

"Doctor, doctor, I keep thinking there are two of me."
"Don't both talk at once."

"Doctor, doctor, I keep painting myself gold."
"You have a gilt complex."

"Doctor, doctor, I think I'm an alligator."
"There's no need to snap."

Doctor: "Have your eyes ever been checked?"
Patient: "No, they've always been blue."

"Doctor, doctor, my son has swallowed a bullet."
"Well don't point him at me then."

What do you call an anesthetist
in a rabbit suit?
The ether bunny

What do you call a doctor
with eight arms?
Doctopus

What do you call a roman
emperor with flu?
Julius Sneezer

What kind of teeth do
you get for a dollar?
Buck teeth

What do you say when the Statue of Liberty sneezes?
God bless America

Idiot: "What did the x-ray of my head show?"
Doctor: "Absolutely nothing."

Idiot: "How long can a person live without a brain?
Doctor: "I don't know, how old are you?"

Idiot: "I need to loose 20 pounds of excess weight fast."
Doctor: "Alright, I'll cut you head off."

"Doctor, doctor, I've just been bitten
on the arm by a werewolf."
"Did you put anything on it?"
"No he seemed to like it as it was."

"Doctor, doctor i've got
a split personality."
"Sit down, both of you."

"Doctor, doctor, I feel like a tortoise."
"Don't worry we'll soon have you out of your shell."

What can run but not walk?
Your nose

What do you call a girl with one leg shorter than the other?
Eileen

Why did the orange go to the doctor?
It wasn't peeling well

What did the judge say to the dentist?
"Do you promise to pull the tooth, the whole tooth, and nothing but the tooth?"

Why did the window see the doctor?
It was having panes

How did the boy get Egyptian flu?
He caught it from his mummy

How did the patient get to hospital so fast?
He flu

How many knees do you have?
Four – your right knee, your left knee and two kid-knees

What did one eye say to the other?
"Between you and me something smells."

What did the doctor give the patient with a splitting headache?
Glue

What do you call children's knees?
Kidneys

What do you call two doctors?
Pair-a-medics

Why are false teeth like stars?
They only come out at night

What did the dentist give to the brass band?
A tuba toothpaste

Why did the leaf go to the doctor?
It was feeling green

Doctor: "I'm afraid I can't do anything about your condition, it's hereditary."
Patient: "In that case send the bill to my parents."

What are apricots?
Where the baby monkeys sleep

Customer: "Have you got asparagus?"
Shopkeeper: "No, we don't sell sparrows and my name's not Gus."

Why did the coffee taste like mud?
Because it was ground this morning

How do you make a lemon drop?
Let go of it

Why did the potato go out with the mushroom?
Because he was fungi to be with

Wife: "Be careful dear, most accidents happen in the kitchen."
Husband: "I know, I have to eat them."

Why do oranges cover themselves in suntan lotion?
Because otherwise they peel

Which country has a very good appetite?
Hungary

What do you get if cross
an apple with a shellfish?
A crab apple

How do you make an apple puff?
Chase it around the garden

How do you make an apple turnover?
Roll it down a hill

How did the girl drown in her bowl of muesli?
She was pulled under by a strong currant

Why did the baker work so hard?
He kneaded the dough

Why are bananas never lonely?
Because they hang around in bunches

Why did the banana go out with the fig?
Because he couldn't find a date

What's green on the outside and
yellow on the inside?
A banana disguised as a cucumber

Why are chefs cruel?
Because they beat eggs, batter fish, and whip cream

What should you do if a gorilla joins your picnic?
Give him the biggest bananas

"Waiter, waiter, this lobster only has one claw."
"It must have been in a fight, sir."
"Then bring me the winner."

"Waiter, waiter, my lunch is talking."
"Well, you did ask for a tongue sandwich, sir."

Where is the best place for
button mushrooms?
On a jacket potato

What was Noah doing in the kitchen?
Preserving pears

What do you get if you cross an
orange with a comedian?
Peels of laughter

"Waiter, waiter, will my pizza be long?"
"No, it will be flat and round."

"Waiter, waiter, why is my meringue all crushed?"
"You did ask me to step on it, sir."

....

Why do toadstools grow so close together?
They don't need mushroom

....

What did one strawberry say to the other strawberry?
"How did we get into this jam?"

....

What stays hot in the refrigerator?
Mustard

....

"Waiter, waiter, this egg is bad."
"Don't blame me, sir, I only laid the table."

....

How do you mend a broken pumpkin?
With a pumpkin patch

....

How do you make a sausage roll?
Push it down a slope

....

Knock, knock.
Who's there?
Lettuce
Lettuce who?
Lettuce in, I've forgotten my key

Knock, knock
Who's there?
Artichokes
Artichokes who?
Artichokes when he eats too fast

What do you call a raspberry that's been run over?
A traffic jam

"Waiter, waiter, bring me a snack and make it snappy."
"Here's your crocodile sandwich, sir."

What's red, green, yellow and orange and wears boxing gloves?
Fruit punch

Why did the boy put sugar on his pillow?
He wanted sweet dreams

"Waiter, waiter, there's a gravestone in my salad."
"No, sir, it's a tomb-ato."

Why did the restaurant owner hire the acrobats?
He needed some tumblers on the table

Did Adam and Eve have a date?
No, they had an apple

What's red and flashes?
A tomato with a loose connection

What's yellow and swings from cake to cake?
Tarzipan

"Waiter, waiter! There's a fly in the butter."
"Yes sir, it's a butterfly."

What's the difference between a nice young lady and a fresh loaf?
One's a well-bred maid and the other is well-made bread

What's a fungi?
A mushroom that likes having fun

Why do waiters prefer elephants to flies?
Have you ever heard anyone complain that there's an elephant in their soup?

How do you make a Mexican chilli?
Send him to the North Pole

Knock, knock
Who's there?
Phil
Phil who?
Phil this cup up with sugar, would you?

Knock, knock
Who's there?
Egbert
Egbert who?
Egbert no bacon, thanks

Why did the boy stare at the orange squash bottle?
It said "concentrate."

How can you spell candy with two letters?
C and Y

Where did the lemonade take the cola?
To a pop concert

"Waiter, waiter there's a fly in my soup."
"I'm sorry, I didn't know you were a vegetarian."

What sort of cake can you eat in the bath?
A sponge

Why did the banana refuse to fight the apple?
Because it was yellow

What is red and cheeky?
Tomato sauce

What is corny and cheeky?
Cheese sauce

How do you make gold soup?
Put 14 carots in it

Did you hear about the couple
that called their baby Caffeine?
It kept them awake all night

Why didn't the banana snore?
It didn't want to wake up the
rest of the bunch

What gives us milk but only has one horn?
A milk truck

Which letter of the alphabet is also a vegetable?
P

Which letter of the alphabet is also a drink?
T

What word only has three letters but is longer than cat?
Banana

What do you call stolen candy?
Hot chocolate

What did the hamburger name his daughter?
Patty

What happened to the laughing egg?
It cracked up

Knock, knock
Who's there?
Cash
Cash who?
Your nuts!

What's green and sings?
Elvis Parsley

What do you get if you add the circumference and diameter of a pumpkin?
Pumpkin pi

How do you start a pudding race?
Sago

What fish do you eat with ice cream?
Jelly fish

What do you call a woman who's sitting on a slice of toast?
Marge

Why was the boy who had the cake upset?
Because it was a stomach cake

Why was the butcher worried?
His job was at steak

Which artist invented fizzy pop?
Lemonado da Vinci

Which Russian leader was round and purple?
Alexander the Grape

What organ is curry good for?
Your tikka

Which building is made from bread, cheese and tomatoes?
The Leaning Tower of Pizza

What do you get if you eat onions and baked beans?
Tear gas

What do you get if you cross a biscuit with a tuxedo?
A smart cookie

What do you get if you put honey on a chair?
Sticky buns

Why are eggs overrated?
Because they're not all
they're cracked up to be

Why are sausages rude?
Because they spit when you cook them

Which vegetables do you find in the toilet?
Peas and leeks

Which vitamin tastes of salt?
Vitamin C

Why didn't the sesame seed leave the casino?
It was on a roll

Why did the pickle stay in bed?
He felt dill

What pie can fly?
A magpie

What should you say before you eat your salad?
Lettuce pray

Why do the French eat snails?
They don't like fast food

Knock, knock
Who's there?
Dishes
Dishes who?
Dish is me, who ish you?

Knock, knock
Who's there?
Juicy
Juicy who?
Juicy me? I see you

Knock, knock
Who's there?
Beetroot
Beetroot who?
Beetroot to yourself

What do you call a pickle
that draws?
A dillustrator

What do you call five bottles of cola?
A pop group

....

What do you call a rich melon?
A melon-aire

....

What do you call fake spaghetti?
Impasta

....

What do you call a rifle with three barrels?
A trifle

....

What was the name of the man who went to the party dressed as a sandwich?
Roland Butter

....

What do you call a peeled potato?
Spuddy in the nuddy

....

Why did the apple cry?
Its peelings were hurt

Where do you learn to make ice-cream?
Sundae school

Why is money called dough?
Because we all knead it

What does a vegetarian waiter earn?
A celery

Why did the boy think his clock was hungry?
It went back four seconds

What did the pickle say when it wanted to play cards?
"Dill me in."

What do you get when two bananas meet?
Banana shake

If a butcher is six foot tall what does he weigh?
Meat

How do you stop milk turning sour?
Keep it in the cow

Why did the doughnut go to the dentist?
To get a jam filling

How do you spell hard water using only three letters?
Ice

"Waiter, waiter, I want a quick snack what do you recommend?"
"Runner beans."

"Waiter, waiter, I'd like to know what's in the stew."
"I don't think you would, sir."

"Waiter, waiter, what's this fly in my soup?"
"I don't know sir, I'm a waiter not a botanist."

"Waiter, waiter, is there soup on the menu?"
"Yes sir, but I can wipe it off for you if you'd like."

"Waiter, waiter, has the chef got pig's feet?"
"I don't know sir, he's wearing shoes."

"Waiter, waiter, your thumb's in my soup."
"It's alright sir, it's not hot."

What do you call a lazy baker?
A loafer

"Waiter, waiter, you're not fit to serve a pig."
"I'm trying my best sir."

"Waiter, waiter, there's a spider in my soup."
"It's alright sir, it's just catching the flies."

Who wrote a book called The Greedy Man?
Buster Gutt

Who wrote a book called 'The 30-Stone Lady'?
Aida Lott

Why didn't the hotdog star in the movie?
The roll wasn't good enough

Why did the woman wear a
helmet at the dinner table?
She was on a crash diet

What begins with T, ends in T,
and is filled with tea?
A teapot

What did the chef give to his girlfriend when he asked her to marry him?
An onion ring

What month is good on toast?
Jam-uary

Why was the tomato red?
Because it saw the salad dressing

Which vitamin helps your eyes?
Vitamin C

What do you get when you cross your dinner with a necklace?
A food chain

Why did the cookie go to the doctor?
Because he was feeling crummy

What did the chef name his son?
Stew

What candy is never on time?
Choco-late

What are two things you don't eat for lunch?
Breakfast and dinner

Why is Swiss cheese served at church?
Because it's holey

What did the girl do after she drank eight sodas?
She burped seven up

Which nut sounds like a sneeze?
A cashew

What did Popeye say to the sweet potato?
"I yam what I yam."

What country does sugar come from?
Sweeten

What's the difference between the sun and bread?
The sun rises from the east and bread rises from the yeast

Where would you find
salad in a clothes shop?
In the dressing room

Why were the strawberries upset?
Because they were in a jam

What room has no walls,
windows, floors or ceilings?
A mushroom

Why did Mrs Grape leave Mr Grape?
She was tired of raisin kids

Why didn't the two fours want any dinner?
They already eight

"Waiter, waiter this soup tastes funny."
"Then why aren't you laughing?"

Did you hear about the fight in the chip shop?
Two fish got battered

Did you hear the secret about the butter?
I won't tell you, you might spread it

What did the cake say to the knife?
"You wanna piece of me?"

What did the gum say to the shoe?
"I'm stuck on you."

What do ghosts put on their bagels?
Scream cheese

What is green and makes holes?
A drill pickle

What is the best thing to put in a pie?
Your teeth

What kind of pie can fly?
A magpie

What kind of soup never gets hot?
Chilli soup

What is a pretzel's
favorite dance?
The twist

Why did the boy put peanut butter on the road?
To go with the traffic jam

How is a banana skin like music?
Because if you don't C sharp you will B flat

What is the most musical part of a turkey?
The drumstick

What vegetable is essential to good music?
The beet

What did Obi-Wan say to Luke when they were eating lunch?
"Use the forks, Luke."

What do you call a frozen policeman?
A cop-sicle

Which hero lives in a bowl?
Souperman

What did one egg say to the other egg?
"Lets get cracking."

Food**

Why did the man put his money
in the freezer?
He needed some cold hard cash

What did one plate say to the other?
"Lunch is on me."

Who serves ice cream faster than a speeding bullet?
Scooperman

What did the snowman eat for breakfast?
Snowflakes

Why is it a bad idea to write on an empty stomach?
Because it's much better to write on paper

When can you put pickles in a door?
When it's ajar

What did the grape do
when it got trodden on?
Let out a little wine

What do you call a woman
with a food mixer on her head?
Belinda

"Waiter, waiter, there's a dead fly in my soup."
"Oh no! Who's going to look after his family?"

What's the difference between bogeys and sprouts?
You can't get kids to eat sprouts

What did the madman walk along?
The psycho-path

"Waiter, waiter, there's a fly in my soup."
"Don't worry, sir, the spider in your roll will get it."

What happened to the comedian who performed for a bunch of cannibals?
He went down well

Why did the baker's hands smell?
Because he kneaded a poo

"Waiter, waiter, there's a dead beetle in my soup."
"Yes, sir, beetles are terrible swimmers."

What did the cockroach say to the beetle?
"Stop bugging me."

What do you do when your nose goes on strike?
Picket

"What is a cannibal's favorite food?
Baked beings

What did the cannibal say when he was full?
"I couldn't eat another mortal."

What did the cannibal have for breakfast?
Buttered host

Why did the cannibal live on his own?
He was fed up with other people

"Waiter, waiter, why is there a cockroach in my soup?"
"Sorry, sir, but we ran out of flies."

What smells of fish and goes around and around at 100 miles per hour?
A goldfish in a blender

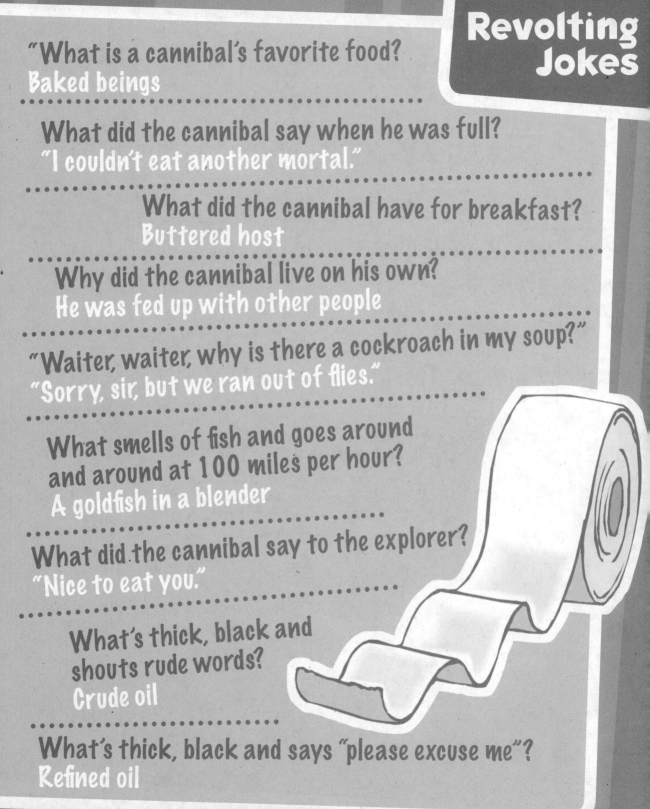

What did the cannibal say to the explorer?
"Nice to eat you."

What's thick, black and shouts rude words?
Crude oil

What's thick, black and says "please excuse me"?
Refined oil

What's the hardest part about sky diving?
The ground

What did the bath say to the toilet?
"You look flushed."

What's invisible and smells like carrots?
Rabbit farts

What do you call the pink bits between a shark's teeth?
Slow swimmers

What has two gray legs and two brown legs?
An elephant with the runs

Boy: "Mummy, can I lick the bowl?"
Mother: "No, just flush like everyone else."

Knock, knock
Who's there?
Gotta
Gotta who?
Gotta go to the toilet!

What did the best man at the cannibal wedding do?
Toasted the bride and groom

What's red and stupid?
A blood clot

What are a cannibal's favorite cookies?
Chocolate fingers

Why don't cannibals eat weathermen?
They give them wind

What did the cannibal make of his new neighbor?
Casserole

What is a cannibal's favorite game?
Swallow the leader

What is the best way to stop acid indigestion?
Don't drink acid

What do you call an American
with a lavatory on his head?
John

Why did Henry VIII have so many wives?
He liked to chop and change

Why didn't the cannibal have any friends?
He kept having them for lunch

Why don't cannibals
eat clowns?
Because they taste
funny

Knock, knock
Who's there?
Snot
Snot who?
Snot you again

Why did Tigger stick his head down the toilet?
He was looking for Pooh

What do you call a woman with two toilets on her head?
Lulu

What do you call a man with a lorry on his head?
Dead

What nut do you find in the toilet?
Pee-nut

Whats red, green and sloppy?
A frog in a liquidizer

First girl: "Your brother is spoiled."
Second girl: "No, he always smells like that."

My brother was made upside down,
his nose runs and his feet smell.

Husband: "Will you still love me when I'm old, smelly and ugly?"
Wife: "Of course I do."

What's old pink and wrinkled and belongs to grandma?
Grandpa

Knock, knock
Who's there?
Abbey
Abbey who?
Abbey stung me on the bum

Knock, knock
Who's there?
Ahab
Ahab who?
Ahab to go to the toilet, let me in quick!

Knock, knock
Who's there?
Alec
Alec who?
Alec to pick my nose

Knock, knock
Who's there?
Doughnut
Doughnut who?
Doughnut go in the toilet, it stinks

Knock, knock
Who's there?
Canoe
Canoe who?
Canoe flush the toilet, please?

Knock, knock
Who's there?
I'm Colin
I'm Colin who?
I'm Colin the doctor because I've got the runs

Knock, knock
Who's there?
Daisy
Daisy who?
Daisy that you smell but I don't believe them

What do you call a girl
who never uses a tissue?
Greensleeves

Knock, knock
Who's there?
Ivan
Ivan who?
Ivan itchy butt

Knock, knock
Who's there?
Ooze
Ooze who?
Ooze made the seat all wet?

Knock, knock
Who's there?
Luxemburg
Luxemburg who?
Luxemburg just pooped
on your shoulder

Knock, knock
Who's there?
Weed
Weed who?
Weed in my trousers again

Knock, knock
Who's there?
Saul
Saul who?
Saul over your shoes, wipe
them before you come in

What happened to the thief who stole some prunes?
He was on the run for weeks

How do poops greet each other?
How do you do-do

What do hangmen read?
Noose papers

Why did the cannibal join the police force?
He liked to grill suspects

Where do young cannibals go to school?
Eton

Did you hear the joke about the cesspit?
It takes a while to sink in

What happened to the man who lit a match by a gas leak?
He rests in pieces

What did one fly say to the other?
"Excuse me is this stool taken?"

"Do you like warts?"
"No."
"Don't worry they'll grow on you."

Why did the lady cannibal join the dating agency?
She wanted to meet edible bachelors

What do you call frozen water?
Ice
What do you call frozen cream?
Ice cream
What do you call frozen tea?
Iced tea
What do you call frozen ink?
Iced ink
Urgh, you had better go take a shower then

What is brown and furry on the inside and white on the outside?
A rat sandwich

What did the executioner do with his pen and paper?
Wrote his chopping list

What's green and fluffy?
A seasick kitten

What do you find up a clean nose?
Fingerprints

Did you hear about the man who was so fat, when he stepped on the scales they said "to be continued"?

If you want to kiss your honey but her nose is runny, you might think it's funny but it's snot

What did the cannibal call the man in the hammock?
Breakfast in bed

What is Beethoven doing in his grave?
De-composing